This book is dedicated to the glory and pleasure of God.

May He use it as He sees fit in the lives of our grandsons
Zeke, Ben, Eli, Jo, Zach, and Gabe, as well as others
of their generation and those who follow.

May they live like real men.

ACKNOWLEDGMENTS

I thank God…

for the two women who have shaped and influenced me the most: my wife, Jera, who has lived this spiritual journey with me for more than 35 years; and my mom, Catherine, who has cheered for Jera and me through it all. Ladies, this book is your sweat and tears as much as it's mine.

for my three children by birth: Missy, Jon, and Ron. You have been the proving grounds of all this book contains. You make me proud. Josh, Rebecca, and Kelsea (my three children by marriage), you are the first-line benefactors of this book. I pray that it brings you continual blessing.

for the "real men" who stood in the gap and lived Jesus Christ before me: You took God seriously and lived well. Your fingerprints are all over my life and this book. You are the men of First Baptist Church in Hemet, Grace Bible Church in Battlement Mesa, Monument View Bible Church in Fruita, Cornerstone Church in Simi Valley, and Revive Church in Brooklyn Park.

THE MAN CODE

MARK HENRY

HARVEST HOUSE PUBLISHERS
EUGENE. OREGON

Cover design by Faceout Studio, Elisha Zepeda

Cover images © Paul El-Tawil, jessicahyde / Shutterstock

Interior design by KUHN Design Group

For bulk, special sales, or ministry purchases, please call 1-800-547-8979.
Email: CustomerService@hhpbooks.com

The Man Code
Copyright © 2024 by Mark Henry
Published by Harvest House Publishers
Eugene, Oregon 97408
www.harvesthousepublishers.com

ISBN 978-0-7369-9003-5 (pbk)
ISBN 978-0-7369-9004-2 (eBook)

Library of Congress Control Number: 2023947117

Printed in the United States of America

24 25 26 27 28 29 30 31 32 / VP / 10 9 8 7 6 5 4 3 2 1

CONTENTS

PART 12: REAL MEN LOVE THE GOSPEL AND THE CHURCH

HOW GOD MADE MEN

*T*he *Man Code* has been a personal journey. In one way, it started when I became a follower of Jesus and began to devote myself to His Word. But in another sense, the journey goes back to something that happened when I was five years old: My father committed suicide.

At that age, I couldn't possibly understand what he had done. Decades later, I still don't understand. But now I have an adult Christian perspective; that makes all the difference how I respond to his action.

Beginning with such pain, you might expect *The Man Code* journey to be a sad one. Instead, it has been a voyage of joyful discovery and fulfillment. The terrible beginning pushed me to seek out God's perspective on the role of the human male in His creation. What I found is both inspiring and rewarding.

In this book, I often use the term *real men* because it carries a powerful connotation in our culture. Two boys look at a ditch. One jumps across it. The other looks at the width of the ditch with trepidation. The first boy says, "Come on! Jump it. Be a man!" We all know what he means. "Be brave. Be strong. Have some backbone." Interestingly, the apostle Paul gave a similar admonishment in 1 Corinthians

16:13-14: "Act like men, be strong." Though Paul was writing to both male and female believers, he made a connection here between manhood and being strong.

Beyond having one X and one Y chromosome and being strong, the most important aspect of being a real man is being a man of God. As creator, God designed men a certain way, and any man who follows that design is a real man. He hears God's call, embraces Jesus as Lord, lives for God's purpose, stays focused, acts with duty and responsibility, practices godly character, uses his strength to protect others, works with diligence, respects authority, cheers and cultivates his family, and advances the work of God. This is the man God has created and called you to be.

God also created women with strength, courage, and backbone, just as He did men. There are similarities between the sexes as well as differences. Nevertheless, the differences are real. They are many, and they are wonderful, and God has purposes behind them. It's unfortunate that society is obsessed with erasing those differences. In doing so, it is going against God's design.

The fact there are differences doesn't mean God values one or the other more highly. God loves all women and men the same. In His eyes, they have equal value. They are equally important. But to understand God's callings in our lives, we must recognize the differences He has created in men and women.

Today's culture takes great pride in telling people, "Be yourself"— but not when it comes to the distinctives God created in men and women. Society tells girls that they should act like boys. And it tells boys they should act like girls. And the result is a lot of confusion that is detrimental—sometimes to the point of mental illness.

Men and women are different. We should not discourage those differences. We should celebrate them. In contrast, society celebrates diversity in almost every area but this. It denies male-female diversity.

Common sense confirms it, but the thought police tell us it is sexist even to mention such differences. This denial of basic truth concerning the sexes does terrible things to both men and women, and even worse things to boys and girls.

There is nothing wrong with being a man. There is nothing wrong with being a woman. We should embrace and enjoy how God made us. This was His plan from the beginning.

This book addresses God's call on men specifically. That's not meant as a slight to women, but as a help to everyone.

Help, LORD, for the godly man ceases to be,
for the faithful disappear from among the sons of men.
PSALM 12:1

I'm not sure we have the men to defend
America from foreign threats any longer.
ARMY SERGEANT

I cannot find a good man to marry.
28-YEAR-OLD WOMAN

I interviewed ten men today for the job, but
I don't think any of them know how to work.
BUSINESS OWNER

Is there a good man who could mentor my son?
SINGLE MOM

I cannot find a good man to lead
a Bible study or serve as an elder.
LOCAL PASTOR

1

WE HAVE A CRISIS

Popular media portrays men in many negative ways. Sitcoms, TV commercials, and even comic books depict men as weak, inept, bumbling, unreliable, greedy, irate, selfish, dangerous, unfit for authority, and stupid. In general, they show masculinity as toxic, even deadly.

Belittling men is popular, modern, and trendy. Tell a joke about men's incompetence or laziness, and you are sure to get a laugh. Tell a similar joke about women, and society will label you as politically incorrect and a hater.

At most major universities, the field of gender studies is more about bashing males than about the objective study of the complexities related to maleness and femaleness. Students are taught to see men and boys as entitled and oppressive.

But, in fact, they are in crisis.

DIMENSIONS OF THE CRISIS

You may have heard that in school, girls do better in courses that require verbal skills, and boys do better in math and science. That used to be true. But now, girls do better than boys in every academic discipline.[1] It's not that girls have improved, but that boys have declined. That decline raises the huge question of why. And we had better find the answers because nothing less than the future of human civilization is at stake.

National Public Radio (NPR) reports, "A new study shows that when it comes to the classroom, girls rule. They outperform boys in math, science, and reading in 70 percent of the 70-plus countries and regions surveyed by the Organization for Economic Cooperation and Development. Girls do better even in countries that rank low on the UN's [United Nation's] gender equality index."[2]

According to the US Department of Education, 134 women graduate from college for every 100 male graduates.[3] And it's not just bachelor's degrees. Bloomberg reports, "As of 2017, women between ages 18 and 24 earned more than two-thirds of all master's degrees, meaning there were 167 women with master's degrees for every 100 men."[4]

It's great that women are getting degrees in large numbers. But the growing imbalance between males and females raises an obvious question: What's going on with men and boys? Closer examination shows that the problem goes far deeper than education. In general, boys are in trouble. So are their adult counterparts.

Dr. Warren Farrell, a prominent author and educator, says that a major part of the problem is what he calls "dad-deprived boys." At a Marin County TEDx event in 2016, he said, "Prisons are basically centers for dad-deprived boys. In California since 1980, we've built 18 new prisons…There has been a 700 percent increase in the prison population of the United States since 1972. That's a 93 percent male population, mostly a dad-deprived boy population."[5]

There have been 389 school shootings since the Columbine incident in 1999. During that time, "more than 357,000 students have experienced gun violence," according to *The Washington Post*.[6]

Males perpetrated almost all of them. Some people see gun control as the solution. But at best, that would be a Band-Aid. It does not address the deeper issue. Guns are not new, but pervasive numbers of school shootings are new. What changed? Specifically, what changed for boys?

EPIDEMIC OF DESPAIR

Many blame school shootings on mental illness. But that begs another question: Why is there a mental health crisis in the United States and in other first world countries? According to the National Alliance on Mental Illness, in 2020, 22.8 percent of American adults had been diagnosed with some form of mental illness.[7] That's one in five!

Don't forget how far society has lowered the bar in this area. There are people who now consider it healthy and normal for a boy to think he is a girl, and vice versa.

Society answers by addressing the symptoms, or by lowering the standards of what is considered normal. To use Senator Daniel Patrick Moynihan's memorable phrase, society is "defining deviancy down."[8] Shouldn't we be asking if society took some wrong turns somewhere along the way?

Even before the COVID-19 pandemic, the United States was spending almost 18 percent of its entire gross domestic product on healthcare. For decades, we spent wildly to cure diseases, make better medicines, build a better healthcare infrastructure, and create better health technology. You would expect this massive amount of money and this many medical advances to pay off in longer and healthier lives. But in 2015, life expectancy for Americans began decreasing.[9] As of this writing, it continues to fall.

Why did life expectancy for Americans start decreasing five years *before* the COVID-19 pandemic? The answer can be described as an epidemic of despair.

The Centers for Disease Control and Prevention (CDC) blames the decline on the rise in drug overdoses, an ever-growing number of suicides, and increased liver disease (this last one is attributed to increased alcohol consumption). People are using drugs and alcohol in an attempt to self-medicate against despair. Suicide is despair on steroids.

Americans—especially men and boys—are dying younger because hopelessness and despair are killing them.

Before age nine, girls and boys commit suicide at about the same low rate. But between the ages of 10 and 14, nearly four times as many boys as girls commit suicide.[10] Between the ages of 15 and 19, boys kill themselves 3.31 times more than girls.[11] For young adults, that number jumps to more than four times![12]

SEEKING MALE ROLE MODELS

Almost everyone agrees that one major problem is the lack of male role models in boys' lives. That makes the problem self-perpetuating. Absent men in one generation create more absent men in the next— and so on. We can stop the cycle, but only if we address it.

Even when fathers are in the picture, they are not always present for their sons. Among boys who have dads in their lives, the boys talk to their fathers an average of 30 *minutes* a week.[13] Meanwhile, boys spend an average of 44 *hours* a week on their phones, watching television, on computers, and with other kinds of electronic screens.[14]

Boys will find role models. If dad doesn't do the job, someone else will. In other words, if you don't want the latest celebrity to serve as your child's mentor, don't hand him the job.

Because boys are prone to imitate the latest sports or media stars, it's important to think about what they learn from them. Negative values, attitudes, and behaviors are likely to be copied unless a parent steps in and teaches boys what is right versus what is wrong.

WHAT WE SOW IN BOYS, WE REAP IN MEN

Educators, clergymen, sociologists, and psychologists have been talking about a crisis among boys for decades. By now, the boy-crisis has become a man-crisis. Large numbers of men haven't grown up. In some cases, it's because they never learned responsibility. In other cases, they've never been taught how to make good or right decisions. They have significant problems with pornography[15] and video game addictions.[16] Some either still live with mom and dad or are too dependent on them.

Dr. Farrell, political scientist and author, describes boys and young men as being in "present hedonistic"[17] mode. Dictionary.com defines a *hedonist* as "a person whose life is devoted to the pursuit of pleasure and self-gratification." If someone's time perspective is "present hedonist," that person is all about the pursuit of pleasure and self-gratification *right now*. In that mode, they seek immediate pleasure and avoid sacrifice or difficulty. They rarely plan for a future beyond the next few hours, and they do not prepare for contingencies. They have no long-term plans. They are rudderless.

Boys and men are in a terrible downward spiral. The crisis is self-perpetuating and multiplying.

ANSWERS

Thankfully, with God's help, we can stop the downward spiral and the cycle of absent dads and broken boys. But we need to face the problem squarely. To one degree or another, it affects the lives of many others. We cannot sustain our present level of civilization without a major turnaround. In biblical terms, *turnaround* means "repentance."

We need a return to the biblical definition of manhood, and we need it now!

Be on the alert, stand firm in the faith,
act like men, be strong.
I CORINTHIANS 16:13

A man's got to have a code,
a creed to live by, no matter his job.[1]
JOHN WAYNE

A Cadet will not lie, cheat, steal,
or tolerate those who do.[2]
WEST POINT CADET HONOR CODE

Duty, Honor, Country.[3]
GENERAL DOUGLAS MACARTHUR

2

TO THE
(MAN) CODE!

My father's death created a deep need in me to understand God's definition of manhood. When I was about 14 and a new Christian, I had a series of encounters with an interesting group of men. They were all in their thirties and forties, and all ex-Marines. They were combat veterans and tougher than nails. They had seen and survived unspeakable things. They had overcome fear and pain.

On one occasion, we sat together in a garage, and I listened to their stories. In combat, they could do (and had done) astounding things. As a teen, their attitudes, talk, and masculinity captivated my imagination. I admired them, and there was much to admire. And as a new Christian, I had already come across 1 Corinthians 16:13: "Be on the alert, stand firm in the faith, act like men, be strong." The phrase "act like men" intrigued me.

As I listened to the guys talking in the garage, I compared "act like men" with what I was hearing. I thought "act like men" had to include physical bravery. These men were loaded with that. They had laid their lives on the line for their country and their families. More than just warriors, they were warriors with a purpose: the freedom, safety, and well-being of a nation.

Looking at them that day in the garage, battlefield glory seemed far away. And sadly, they had reduced manliness to drinking, getting drunk, and seducing women. I will always admire certain aspects of their lives. But on that day, through God's grace, I began to see the truth. They were broken.

KEY ELEMENTS OF THE MAN CODE

God's admonition to "act like men" had to mean more. I went back to the Bible, determined to know God's definition of manhood. That's when I began to work on what I now call "the Man Code." I wanted to know what God expects of a man. Because the Bible is timeless, God's expectation of men would involve more than the latest trends. Merely inspirational or influential would not cut it. The principles of real manhood had to be *transformational*.

I didn't want to rely on my own ideas or clever things I came up with. Whatever I came up with needed to be better than that—infinitely better. Ideas I might dream up would make me yet another blind guide trying to lead the blind (Matthew 15:14). I wanted God's own guidance. He is our Designer and Maker. So the ideas and principles had to be *biblical*.

They also needed to be *transferable* to others. It could not be one and done. I wanted truths and principles I could transfer to other men, as well as to my sons.

Transformational

For millions of men, something's missing. Something's gone wrong. Vast numbers of men feel confused, weary, guilty, and depressed. They need more than a pep talk to make things right. They need more than another drink, or another hit. Men need purpose and focus. They need something real and powerful—real enough and powerful enough to transform them. And that transformation needs to last.

Mere surface change is insufficient. A new façade will not do. We need something that reworks our basic structure—the foundation and framing. To be transformed means to become something new.

Biblical

The most important element of the Man Code is that it is based on God's truth. The world doesn't need another exercise in feeling good. We need answers from God Himself. They must come from God's own Word.

The central character of the Bible is Jesus. He's also the central character of history. Voices shouting opinions are not rare. A pandemonium of ideas, words, impressions, fears, hatreds, loves, and passions saturates the world. But Jesus stands above all that. He alone spoke as God in human flesh. He alone, of all people from all times, died and rose from the dead, never to die again. He solved mankind's problem—separation from God due to sin. He made it possible for us to come back to God.

John 1:1 calls Jesus the Word. John 1:3 says He is the creator of all things. Then, in verse 14, we read, "The Word became flesh."

To be biblical means to be built on Him.

Transferable

As I wrote the Man Code, I realized it not only needed to be transformational and biblical, but also contagious. During pandemics, experts tell us we must "slow the spread." But when it comes to the Man Code, we need to "speed up the spread"!

Though we are individuals, we cannot assume that what we do only affects us and not others. We have family and friends. Many people surround us. To be meaningful, the Man Code must take in consideration our impact on them. Every man has a sphere of influence. It's great when a man becomes new, better, happier, and more fulfilled. But that change is best when it has a positive influence on others, especially a man's own children.

CHILDREN AND THE CODE OF THE WEST

As parents, we transfer values and beliefs to our offspring by how we live and what we say. We pray with our children, encourage them, discipline them, and love them. We take them places and teach them about wise choices. We also influence them by how we play with them.

When my wife, Jera, and I began to have children, we did all the above. But the need for making our values transferable became apparent. We wanted some way of packaging those values and making them compact so they could be picked up by our children.

The need for this became clear to me in 1993. The Walt Disney Company began filming a movie not far from a church in Colorado where I was the pastor. Our family would drive by the area and see sets being built. We later found out this was being done for a film called *Tall Tale*, a story about a 12-year-old boy named Daniel and his dad, Jonas. The dad taught Daniel something he called "the code of the West"—it focused on three values he deemed important for life: caring for the farm, protecting those who are weaker, and acting like a gentleman in front of women and children. The code had a catchy ring to it in the movie.

After we saw the movie, I noticed my two sons playing around the house as if on horseback. I watched them pretend to rope and ride, and sometimes I heard them shout, "The code of the West!"

They remembered the code. The ideas had been transferred!

It struck me that for a code to be transferable, it must be memorable and repeatable. The Marines have a code—*semper fidelis*, a Latin phrase that means "always faithful" or "always loyal." Such codes have been common in all branches of all militaries throughout history. Mothers of Spartan warriors would say to their sons, "Come home *with* your shield, or come home *on* your shield." In other words, "Do not surrender. Come home alive with your shield or dead on it. Be brave to the end!"

I started thinking about what I wanted to live by, and what I wanted to communicate to my children. I began to make a list.

THE MAN CODE

Over the years, I compiled and refined the list to these 12 essential priorities. A real man...

1. Pursues biblical success

2. Possesses focused ambition

3. Assumes responsibility

4. Exhibits godly character

5. Demonstrates consideration

6. Protects others

7. Works with diligence

8. Respects authority

9. Honors his wife

10. Trains his children

11. Does not abandon his family

12. Loves the gospel and the church

You might have noticed the verbs in the Man Code. They are deliberately chosen to show active and ongoing involvement. We don't master these essentials and call it a day. And these are not "pie in the sky" goals for some future day when we have more time or we enter a different stage of life. Instead, this code is continually before us as God's high and holy standard for men, based on the inerrant principles in His Word. We will never outgrow it!

Also, the Man Code is fulfilled in a man when all 12 aspects are functioning simultaneously, and a man is learning and growing in each of these areas. The priorities are numbered for clarity and are not sequential or dependent on mastery of the previous step before moving on to the next. They are all priorities for all time.

As I taught the Man Code to our children, I could sense we were raising the bar for our family. Our sons made this code part of the fabric of their lives. Our daughter took it to heart too. It raised her expectations; this was what she would look for in a husband. Our grown children are now instilling the Man Code in our grandsons.

STUDY QUESTIONS

1. How has the crisis among men and boys touched your own life?

2. Is there a solution?

3. What can you do about this crisis?

4. Everyone lives by a code. What code would you say you are living by? How does it line up with the code as listed on page 23?

5. Who is the author of your code? What is it producing in your life and the lives of those around you?

6. Do you want to abide by the Man Code? If so, start memorizing it. I've provided an easy-to-memorize list of the code on page 23, and again at the end of this book on page 279.

PART 1:

REAL MEN PURSUE BIBLICAL SUCCESS

A wise man heeds the call of God by embracing Christ. His faith manifests itself in actions that align with God's will as expressed in His Word. Such a man actively pursues God's kind of success, knowing that the fruit of such success will last forever.

Be strong and very courageous; be careful to do according to all the law which Moses My servant commanded you; do not turn from it to the right or to the left, so that you may have success wherever you go. This book of the law shall not depart from your mouth, but you shall meditate on it day and night, so that you may be careful to do according to all that is written in it; for then you will make your way prosperous, and then you will have success.

JOSHUA 1:7-8

Waste no more time arguing about what a good man should be. Be one.[1]

MARCUS AURELIUS

Beware the barrenness of a busy life.[2]

SOCRATES

HOW DO YOU
SPELL *SUCCESS?*

The Man Code begins with the pursuit of biblical success. That pursuit raises an important question, and the answer will illuminate every part of this book and should inform every part of our lives: *What is biblical success?*

We commonly define success as "an ambition realized." The Bible—from Genesis to Revelation—is a book about Jesus. Biblical success is realizing the ambition to please the Lord. It is spelled out in 2 Corinthians 5:9, "We have as our ambition, whether at home or absent, to be pleasing to Him."

This is the apex of Christian aspiration. In context, we see that this passage speaks of the contrast between two current states for followers of Christ. "Whether at home or absent" means here on earth or up in heaven. Whether here or there, our Christian ambition stays the same—to please the Lord Jesus. Our chief ambition right now must be the same as the chief ambition we will hold in heaven. It's thrilling to consider that your eternal purpose begins here and now.

PLEASING HIM

Some people hear this idea about success and say that it cannot be that simple. But it *is* that simple. From the moment you become a follower of Jesus, your highest and best ambition is to please Him in everything—whether on earth or in heaven, from that point forward and forevermore. Pleasing Him takes us from the hypothetical "What would Jesus do?" to a real, non-hypothetical question in the present tense: "What *does* Jesus want me to do?"

The Greek word translated "ambition" refers to an overarching theme that constantly resets every priority in its favor. The overarching priority of a Christ follower should be to please the Lord. This is infinitely more satisfying than following a list of dos and don'ts. It is a relationship.

Jesus modeled this allegiance for us. In John 6:38, He said, "I have come down from heaven, not to do My own will, but the will of Him who sent Me."

Jesus Himself is our example. He came to seek and save the lost because it was the will of His Father. He lived to please the Father. It motivated all His actions. Whatever your background or culture, whatever phase of life you are in, whether you are male or female, rich or poor, *biblical success means pleasing God.*

LAWYERS AND PHARISEES

Scripture tells about various people who did not please God. Some were wealthy, some were highly educated, and some even led nations. Many of them stood at the pinnacle of human achievement. Still, they did not please God.

When Jesus was physically on earth, there was a Jewish sect known as the Pharisees. Professing to be the guardians of God's holy Word, by the time Jesus arrived, they had elevated tradition above Scripture. They were educated, financially secure, wielded great political power, and were celebrated for their piety. But even at the top of the religious heap, they missed the purpose of God.

We all want education for our children, but education does not guarantee biblical success. No matter how learned they become, they can still miss the purpose of God. It's the same with money, power, and dozens of other signs of worldly success. You can have everything the world admires while missing the purpose of God. That means you miss the essence of your own purpose. Such a fundamental omission inevitably leads to feelings of disillusionment and meaninglessness. Missing the purpose of God means surviving (for a while) but not flourishing.

Luke 7:30 shows how the Pharisees and scribes (lawyers) missed God's purpose: "The Pharisees and the lawyers rejected God's purpose for themselves, not having been baptized by John."

That may seem strange. What could be so important about following the instructions of a guy who lived in the wilderness and ate bugs? (Matthew 3:4). John's message was important because God sent him to introduce Jesus. In Mark 1:7-8, John said, "After me One is coming who is mightier than I, and I am not fit to stoop down and untie the thong of His sandals. I baptized you with water; but He will baptize you with the Holy Spirit."

John came to "prepare the way of the Lord" (Matthew 3:3 KJV), but many rejected John and his message. That meant rejecting Jesus. And in rejecting Jesus, they rejected God's purpose for their lives.

Even those of us who have accepted Jesus can miss parts of God's purpose for our lives. And wherever we miss the purpose of God, we fail…because biblical success means pleasing God.

YOUR PURPOSE IN THIS GENERATION

One day I walked into my daughter's room. She had written Acts 13:36-37 on a whiteboard. "David, after he had served the purpose of God in his own generation, fell asleep, and was laid among his fathers, and underwent decay; but He whom God raised did not undergo decay."

This is a wonderful passage about the deity of Jesus and His role as Messiah. I had read it countless times. But this time I saw a point I had always missed in the past. God had a specific purpose for David *in his generation*! David died after he served that purpose.

I asked myself, *Will I fulfill God's purpose in the generation in which He has placed me?*

The question has nothing to do with finances, celebrity, or the praise of men. It is not about human titles or honors. People soon forget those things. Real success means living for the pleasure of God. If we live for God's pleasure, it will be manifest in our words, attitudes, and actions. We will serve the purpose of God in our generation.

4

DAVID'S SUCCESS

How did David serve the purpose of God in his generation? Was it his sinless life? No. Though one of the Bible's great heroes, David was also one of its foremost sinners.

David also did great deeds. So, how did he serve the purpose of God in his generation? Was it because of his journey from country boy to king of the country? Was it his military prowess—his skills as a warrior, strategist, or leader of men? Was it his progression from relative poverty to enormous wealth? Was it his ability to grow a poor kingdom into a wealthy one? Did his talent as a poet, songwriter, and musician cause him to serve the purpose of God in his generation?

No. Those were the outgrowths of David's success. His success began in his heart.

FACING GOLIATH

The most famous battle in Jewish history was an unlikely one. It took place in the Valley of Elah, about 15 miles east of Bethlehem. The Israelites encamped on one side of the valley and the Philistines on the other. Every day, a Philistine champion would evoke terror in the hearts of the Israeli soldiers. He would step out from the ranks of the Philistines and challenge Israel. His name was Goliath.

Everything Scripture says about Goliath helps us understand the fear he aroused in Israel's fighting men. The Bible's description begins with a bang: Goliath stood "six cubits and a span" (1 Samuel 17:4). That translates to more than nine-and-a-half feet tall!

Goliath carried a huge spear with an iron tip, wore a large bronze helmet, and a heavy coat of armor weighing 125 pounds. When I first read that as a student, I thought, *No one can carry around that much armor!* According to a 2017 Government Accountability Office report, a US Marine carries an average of 117 pounds into combat. Loads go as high as 140 pounds, and these are for regular-sized men.[1]

Every morning and every evening for 40 days, the giant taunted the forces of Israel:

> Why do you come out to draw up in battle array? Am I not the Philistine and you servants of Saul? Choose a man for yourselves and let him come down to me. If he is able to fight with me and kill me, then we will become your servants; but if I prevail against him and kill him, then you shall become our servants and serve us…I defy the ranks of Israel this day; give me a man that we may fight together (1 Samuel 17:8-10).

SHEPHERD BOY

After the Israelite army put up with 40 days of this verbal abuse, a shepherd boy from Bethlehem arrived. David was too young to fight in the army. His father, Jesse, had sent him to the front lines with provisions for his older brothers. David dropped off the supplies, then saw the troops lined up for battle. He ran to see what was going on.

He arrived in time to see the monstrous man step out from the Philistine ranks. He heard Goliath taunt the soldiers of Israel and blaspheme God.

This outraged David. "Who is this uncircumcised Philistine," he asked, "that he should taunt the armies of the living God?" (verse 26).

David volunteered to fight Goliath. His older brothers and others around him said, in effect, "You haven't even shaved yet, and you expect to go out there and fight that giant?"

David remained undaunted. When the higher-ups got wind of David's determination, they brought him before King Saul. The king said, "You are not able to go against this Philistine to fight with him; for you are but a youth while he has been a warrior from his youth" (verse 33).

David answered by recounting his duties as a shepherd. He had saved a lamb from a bear. On another occasion, he rescued a lamb from a lion's mouth. He said to Saul, "Your servant has killed both the lion and the bear; and this uncircumcised Philistine will be like one of them, since he has taunted the armies of the living God" (verse 36).

David made it clear that he did not expect to defeat the giant in his own strength, but in God's. In verse 37, he said to Saul, "The LORD who delivered me from the paw of the lion and from the paw of the bear, He will deliver me from the hand of this Philistine."

This is crucial. David made God the context and focal point. With God on his side, Goliath ceased to be so big.

SHOWDOWN IN ELAH

Finally, King Saul relented and let David face Goliath. Perhaps he thought the boy's mutilation at the hands of the giant would make his men angry enough to fight. Or maybe he had another plan in mind. But the level of his desperation was obvious.

Saul gave David his own royal armor. The boy put it on and tried to move around, but he had no experience with armor. He chose to face Goliath clothed and armed as what he was—a shepherd. David carried a stick, a sling, and a small bag. He walked down the hillside from where the Hebrew soldiers stood. At the creek near the midpoint between the armies, he picked up five stones and put them in his bag. He crossed the stream as Goliath and his shield bearer walked down the hill from the other side.

In 1 Samuel 17:43 we read, "The Philistine said to David, 'Am I a dog, that you come to me with sticks?' And the Philistine cursed David by his gods."

As he had shown for the last 40 days, Goliath was a master of intimidation. He continued his taunt. "Come to me, and I will give your flesh to the birds of the sky and the beasts of the field" (verse 44).

Goliath's threats did not work on David. The shepherd boy—the real man—answered,

> You come to me with a sword, a spear, and a javelin, but I come to you in the name of the LORD of hosts, the God of the armies of Israel, whom you have taunted. This day the LORD will deliver you up into my hands, and I will strike you down and remove your head from you. And I will give the dead bodies of the army of the Philistines this day to the birds of the sky and the wild beasts of the earth, that all the earth may know that there is a God in Israel, and that all this assembly may know that the LORD does not deliver by sword or by spear; for the battle is the LORD's and He will give you into our hands (verses 45-47).

Neither Zechariah 4:6 nor Romans 8:31 had yet been written, but both were already true. "'Not by might nor by power, but by

My Spirit,' says the LORD of hosts." "What then shall we say to these things? If God is for us, who can be against us?" (NKJV).

THE BATTLE IS THE LORD'S

Goliath lumbered in the direction of the boy, his great spear in his hand. As David moved toward the giant, he put his hand into the bag and pulled out a stone. He placed the stone in the pouch of the sling. Then, as shepherds had done through the centuries, David swung the sling in a wide arc above his head, releasing the stone at tremendous speed. The stone struck Goliath in the forehead and sunk deep into the giant's skull.

According to Jörg Sprave, a German researcher and slingshot enthusiast, slingshot specialists in the Roman army were as accurate as men with guns. The force of the stone was the equivalent of being shot by a .44 Magnum.[2]

David's heart was that of a shepherd—a protector. His actions protected his mom and dad, his brothers, and other members of his family. He protected the soldiers on the hill behind him. He protected King Saul and all Israel. And he protected God's reputation.

Something timeless and intrinsically heroic permeates this story. It connects deeply to men and boys, capturing their imaginations on many levels. Most of all, it connects them to the sense of purpose God placed in them from the beginning.

When my sons were young, I would read this account to them. When I finished, they would say, "Tell us the story again!" Now I tell it to my grandsons. When I get to the end, they say, "Tell us the story again!"

God has His purposes for the men of our generation! Deep down, we all know it. When we hear this story, we realize it anew. Each of us has been singled out by God and called to greatness. But understand that human measures of success do not match God's kind of greatness. David received wealth, fame, and power, but none of these convey his success. We see his success in Acts 13:36: "David... served the purpose of God in his own generation."

David was a success, but not because of his bravery, education, family position, wealth, or career. He was a success because he pleased God. This is the mark of a real man. Real men pursue biblical success.

STUDY QUESTIONS

1. The Pharisees were educated, powerful, and wealthy. How did they fail to be "real men"?

2. David did many amazing deeds in life, but they were not the measure of his success. Pleasing God in those different roles—military general, businessman, king, poet, musician—was the measure. If God spoke to you about your life at this moment, would He call you successful?

3. What grips you the most about the story of David and Goliath?

4. David knew God. How does a man know God? Is it possible to know for sure that you are a child of God and you are going to heaven? What does 1 John 5:12-13 say?

5. Ask yourself the hard questions: Do you bear the marks of a real man? Are you a real success, biblically speaking? What can you do to please God more in the various facets of your life?

PART 2:

REAL MEN POSSESS FOCUSED AMBITION

Men face distractions and diversions on every side. For biblical success, we need focused ambition. That means to live with intentionality. Every area of life requires a measure of planning. That's because life will throw surprises our way. Therefore, the effective execution of our plans requires flexibility and unrelenting focus.

> *Set your mind on the things above, not on the things that are on earth.*
> **COLOSSIANS 3:2**

> *Where jealousy and selfish ambition exist, there is disorder and every evil thing.*
> **JAMES 3:16**

> *The successful warrior is the average man, with laser-like focus.*[1]
> **BRUCE LEE**

> *Great ambition is the passion of a great character. Those endowed with it may perform very good or very bad acts. All depends on the principles which direct them.*[2]
> **NAPOLEON BONAPARTE**

5

MENTAL DISCIPLINE

By place of birth, Nehemiah was Persian. By faith, his home was a city he had never seen—Jerusalem.

His great-grandparents—or perhaps his great-great-grandparents—had been taken from the land of Judah. Nehemiah himself rose to a high position in Persian society. He was powerful, successful, and respected. No one questioned his loyalty to the king. In fact, as the royal cupbearer, it was his job to protect the man who was, at that time, the most powerful ruler in the world.

Then one day, Nehemiah's brother and some others returned from a visit to Jerusalem. In the book that bears his name, Nehemiah recorded their news and his reaction.

> Now it happened in the month Chislev, in the twentieth year, while I was in Susa the capitol, that Hanani, one of my brothers, and some men from Judah came; and I asked them concerning the Jews who had escaped and had survived the captivity, and about Jerusalem. They said

to me, "The remnant there in the province who survived
the captivity are in great distress and reproach, and the
wall of Jerusalem is broken down and its gates are burned
with fire." When I heard these words, I sat down and wept
and mourned for days (Nehemiah 1:1-14).

Have you ever wept and mourned for days? Nehemiah's heart
was broken. Jerusalem, that great city of God, was still in ruins. The
Jews who had returned to the Holy Land to restore Jerusalem were
in distress and reproach. The city's walls were down, leaving God's
people vulnerable to every thug or gang that might come along. The
gates lay in ashes. The enemies of God's people could come and go
as they pleased.

Worst of all, God's name was mocked because of all this. This was
His city. These were His people.

NEHEMIAH'S FOCUS

Nehemiah served as a cupbearer for King Artaxerxes. Today, a cupbearer might sound about three steps below a butler. But in the king's
court of that time, this was a lead position in the king's security detail.
It was much like working in the Secret Service today. Nehemiah's
job was to keep the king alive, to step between him and any danger.

Nehemiah feared God and longed for Him to restore the Jewish
people to the land of Israel. As a child, Nehemiah must have cheered
when he heard about how God had raised up Zerubbabel and 50,000
of his countrymen to return to Israel and rebuild the temple. But on
this day, Nehemiah's heart broke.

What was the big deal? What made this powerful and respected
man weep and mourn for days? In ancient times, the walls of a city
stood as that city's primary line of defense. They allowed people to

live in safety and security from marauding thieves and foreign threats. Good walls secured everything from food to gold to people, including wives and children.

In the case of Jerusalem, Nehemiah saw the walls as a matter of God's reputation. This city was the eternal capital of God's chosen people, the place God chose for His name to be known. For the walls to remain broken and the gates burned meant that every foe, past and present, would continue to mock God's holy name.

Nehemiah knew the walls must be rebuilt. He must have thought, *Someone's got to get this done!* For months, he prayed about the situation. Apparently, during those months, his prayer moved from "Someone's got to get this done!" to "God, let *me* build this wall." And God did just that. After four months of praying, God opened the door with King Artaxerxes. Acting on the authority of the king, Nehemiah would lead an expedition to Jerusalem to rebuild the wall.

Nehemiah laid out a plan, a timeline, and a comprehensive list of required assets. The king and queen granted it all: a diplomatic letter of passage, authority to secure building materials, a military escort, the executive authority to act on behalf of the king, and much more. God put a holy ambition in Nehemiah's heart, opened the door to service, and equipped him for the task.

Ambition is the passion or drive to act. We live in a generation of passivity. Let someone else do it. You see it at the workplace—one person does as little as possible while others carry the load. You see it in families—men who expect their wives to carry the spiritual load or the parenting load. Nehemiah was not content watching others. He was a man of focused ambition, and that gave him the impetus to act.

FOCUS AND AMBITION

After two months on a camel, Nehemiah arrived at the Mount of Olives. He saw Jerusalem and the temple. They were a mess! The walls were in ruins. As he approached from a distance, the people looked like ants living among the rubble.

Nehemiah worked systematically and according to plan. The third night after arriving, he did a personal inspection of the walls. He identified and prioritized what needed to happen and when. He listed the manpower and materials he would need. The task seemed impossible. The Jews sent back earlier had mostly failed to do the job. Nehemiah must have been tempted to despair. Time and again, he must have said to himself, "Steady! Steady as we go! Stay focused. God has this."

The following day, Nehemiah gathered the people of Jerusalem and shared all that God had put on his heart. He spoke passionately about God's leading to build the walls and the support of King Artaxerxes. The people were moved, and they committed themselves to the task.

As the people built the wall, the enemies of God and Israel plotted. Sanballat, Nehemiah's archenemy, was furious (Nehemiah 4:1). He much preferred to keep the Jews as easy prey to pillage. Over the next 52 days, the enemies planned and executed three attacks.

THREE LINES OF ATTACK

First Line of Enemy Attack: Mockery

First, the enemies mocked and threatened these feeble Jews. They said, "If a fox should jump on it, he would break their stone wall down!" (Nehemiah 4:3). Here is the lesson: When you have ambition to do the will of God, Satan will send someone (or even millions of someones) to mock you. Mocking is a tried-and-true way to make men passive, to make them disengage, to get them to cease and desist. If you are doing a good deed for the glory of God in your community, family, work, or church, Satan's thugs will come mocking!

What did Nehemiah do? He prayed that God would hear the mocking, and he stayed focused. He said, "We built the wall and the whole wall was joined together to half its height, for the people had a mind to work" (verse 6).

Second Line of Enemy Attack: Induce Fear

Second, as the enemies of God saw the progress, they mustered an army to attack and kill Nehemiah and his leaders. Even under the threat of war, Nehemiah refused to be distracted. He prayed! He also challenged the people: "When I saw their fear, I rose and spoke to the nobles, the officials and the rest of the people: 'Do not be afraid of them; remember the Lord who is great and awesome, and fight for your brothers, your sons, your daughters, your wives and your houses'" (Nehemiah 4:14).

Then Nehemiah told the people to get weapons! Verse 17 says, "Those who were rebuilding the wall and those who carried burdens took their load with one hand doing the work and the other holding a weapon."

Nehemiah stayed focused, and the building continued.

Third Line of Enemy Attack: Personal Assassination

As the walls neared completion, the enemies of God tried another approach. Plotting an assassination, they invited Nehemiah to meet them. They said they wanted to have a conversation that would lead to peace. Can you hear them? "Let's talk. We want to be your friends." Nehemiah's response was priceless. He sent messengers, saying, "I am doing a great work and I cannot come down. Why should the work stop while I leave it and come down to you?" (6:3).

The enemies sent similar messages to Nehemiah four times, and each time, he answered in the same way. Nehemiah had a vision and he stayed focused on it. He refused to be distracted or diverted. He focused on the task God had laid out for him. Under his leadership, the Jews in Jerusalem rebuilt the walls in just 52 days!

With humans, this was an impossible task. The Jews had failed to rebuild the wall for 50 years. But with God, all things are possible (Matthew 19:26). God used a man with a clear ambition who stayed focused until he got the job done.

Real men stay focused on God's calling. Brother, you will never get started without the ambition, drive, and passion to act. And you will never successfully complete your task without consistent focus on your mission. God does not just want us to start projects; He wants us to finish them!

FINDING GOD'S DIRECTION

One last thought: Ambition not guided in the right direction will destroy you. James 3:14 says, "If you have bitter jealousy and selfish ambition in your heart, do not be arrogant and so lie against the truth."

Selfish ambition results in every evil under the sun—addictions of all kinds, abandoned spouses, affairs, children left without guidance and discipline, people blaspheming Jesus Christ. Ambition, drive, and passion are good when they are guided by the hand of God. That's what happened in Nehemiah's life.

What great thing(s) does God have for you? What work stands before you—glorious work that honors Him, blesses your family and friends, and builds His kingdom? Keep reading. *The Man Code* will help you find God's direction in shaping your ambition, infusing it with His power and dedicating it to His purposes.

6

DEFEATING DISTRACTIONS

Biblical success—that is, pleasing God—does not happen by accident. Biblical success occurs when we have a deliberate ambition and focus. The writer of Hebrews gave his readers a prayer request that revealed his ambition and focus. In Hebrews 13:18, he wrote, "Pray for us, for we are sure that we have a good conscience, desiring to conduct ourselves honorably in all things."

To "conduct ourselves honorably in all things" is the goal. To achieve it, we must stay focused on that goal. The more we do this, the better we get at it. But don't allow yourself to become overconfident. Honorable conduct requires humility.

If you try to keep biblical success in a limited compartment in your life, you won't succeed at consistently honorable conduct. To succeed, you need to orient *everything* toward God. Conduct yourself honorably in *all things*. Don't leave anything out.

We must focus all our choices on our ambition to be biblically successful. Focused ambition means making specific choices that take you toward specific goals. It means doing everything with intentionality.

Make choices with specific purposes in mind. To become a medical doctor, you must, at some point, intend to become a medical doctor. You cannot push through medical school and internships without specific intent and strong resolve.

Spiritual success is the same. God reveals His goals and purposes in the Bible. Use the clarity you find in God's Word and push forward.

Life will pull you in many different directions. That's why intent is not enough. Your ambition needs focus. Becoming a doctor takes natural ability plus years of hard work. And remember that the work must be intentional toward a goal. You can work hard at whittling or playing video games, but neither will make you a doctor. Work patterns can shift easily when you lose focus. Yes, it's necessary for you to put food on the table and meet other more immediate obligations. But never let your focus slip from your overall ambition.

THE 10,000-HOUR RULE

Journalist Malcolm Gladwell helped popularize a concept known as the 10,000-Hour Rule. He based it on a study done by psychologist Anders Ericsson.[1] The idea is that to become great at something, you must practice doing it the right way for about 10,000 hours.

Ericsson himself felt that Gladwell had been too simplistic, leaving out key elements. For instance, Ericsson complained that Gladwell's 10,000 hours did "not even mention the concept of deliberate practice." Ericsson emphasized "goal-directed, deliberate practice"[2]—a fantastic way of viewing focused ambition and intentionality.

To become a piano virtuoso takes thousands of hours practicing and honing skills. But to become great, you can't play "Chopsticks" for thousands of hours. You must work to master one level of difficulty, then push yourself upward to the next. You need to stretch yourself. To grow.

This is true in every area of life. Greatness requires "goal-directed, deliberate practice." Perhaps you don't desire to be a great surgeon, musician, or athlete. But how about being a great dad? Even that takes practice. It takes intention. It takes focused ambition.

For most of us, that means practicing on the job. Your premarital counseling did not include a 10,000-hour course in marriage building or fatherhood. Some people learn a great deal from their own parents, but not everyone has that privilege. And there's always a difference between watching someone else do something, and doing it yourself.

So if you want a great marriage, make it your focused ambition. See every day as an opportunity for "goal-directed, deliberate practice."

HOLDING FOCUS

We live in a world filled with groovy roads. By *groovy*, I don't mean cool or fashionable. I mean roads with actual grooves that grab your tires and pull you in a different direction. How many corrections a minute are your hands making as you fight those grooves?

That's how it is with the fight for your attention and affection. Most of what claims your attention is not evil. Yet the distractions can become devastating if they divert you from the biblical success you seek.

That is why we need intentionality. Focused ambition means that you instigate action. You don't passively react to whatever comes along. You don't merely do whatever feels good in the moment. If you do, Satan will eat you for lunch. Make a thoughtful plan and carry it out.

Proverbs 12:20 says, "Those who plan peace have joy" (ESV). Proverbs also gives everyone—men and women—a wonderful role model in the virtuous woman of chapter 31. She plans every step. She executes that plan with precision. Nothing deters her. As a result, she experiences success at every level of life.

Your plans will be established only when you commit your work to God. Proverbs 16:3 says, "Commit your works to the LORD and your plans will be established." Orient your life and work toward God. Make sure all your successes are His successes. Plan to succeed as a husband, father, in business, and as a Christian. Do you want to be morally pure? Have a plan so that when temptation comes, you will not cave in.

We must keep our eyes on the compass and our focus on true north: pleasing God. Proverbs 15:26 says, "Evil plans are an abomination to the LORD."

Some say, "I'm not a planner." But you would starve if that were entirely true. At some level, everyone is a planner. Nourish that instinct. Proverbs 21:5 says, "The plans of the diligent lead surely to advantage."

BE LIKE YOUR HEAVENLY FATHER

Our churches need exceptional leaders and servants. Our homes need committed husbands and fathers. Our communities need men of faith and integrity. So plan! Be like your Father in heaven. He's a planner. Scripture is full of plans He has made. Jesus said, "Be sons of your Father who is in heaven" (Matthew 5:45). In context, that means, "Be like your heavenly Father."

Romans 8:29 tells us about God's ambition for us. He plans for each of us "to be conformed to the image of His Son." The preceding verse, Romans 8:28, tells us how God enacts His plan for us: "We know that God causes all things to work together for good to those who love God, to those who are called according to His purpose."

What does God use? He uses "all things." How do they work? They "work together." Think about the universe, our salvation, and how God works daily in your life and mine. He chose to involve Himself personally in weaving you together in your mother's womb (Psalm

139:13). God says to each of us, "Before I formed you in the womb, I knew you" (see Jeremiah 1:5). And we can say with the psalmist, "From my mother's womb you have cared for me" (Psalm 71:6 NLT).

God was intentional! When God made you, He had a plan for you...and He still does.

Real men don't chase after the wind, nor are they driven by it. We need clear direction from God. We need mental and emotional focus. Without those things, we cannot win. Stay focused. Stay out of the ditch.

THE MAN WHO RESCUED THE WORLD

The Bible is refreshingly honest about its heroes. We know all kinds of facts about the people who populate its pages—the good, the bad, and the ugly. The Bible shows Moses throwing a temper tantrum. It tells us in painful detail how David became an adulterer and then a murderer. With unrelenting clarity, it gives us a picture of Samson as a self-indulgent womanizer.

Of all the major characters in the Old Testament, only two do not have records of glaring sin: Daniel and Joseph. In many ways, they led similar lives.

Joseph consistently demonstrated faith, did hard work, and exhibited high moral character. He showed a kind of wisdom that comes from not just the knowledge of God, but companionship with God. From this, most people would assume that he came from a perfect family. He did not. To call his family dysfunctional would be a massive understatement! Yet this is the most important family since Adam and Eve. Through this family would come the salvation of the world.

Joseph and his brothers were great-grandsons of Abraham, grandsons of Isaac, and sons of Jacob. God changed Jacob's name to *Israel*. The families of his sons would become the 12 tribes of Israel, also known as the children of Israel, or just Israel. But with only a couple of exceptions, these were not good men.

FAVORITE SON

Joseph was Jacob's favorite son. In moral character, Joseph stood head and shoulders above his brothers. Consequently, they hated him. It didn't help their relationship that Joseph was also smart, winsome, good looking, and utterly convinced of his own future greatness. In his defense, God Himself gave Joseph the knowledge of his glorious future. Joseph, from an early age, learned to discern the voice of God. He had dreams in which his whole family bowed to him. Even his dad didn't like that much. Joseph's older brothers hated him for this.

Through it all, Joseph remained Dad's favorite. At age 13, Jacob gave the boy a spectacular coat—the famous coat of many colors (Genesis 37:3). His brothers seethed.

You can add another item to the brothers' list of grievances. Jacob sometimes used Joseph to check on the brothers and their flocks, then report back. They must have viewed Joseph as a spy who looked over their shoulders as they worked.

GOD'S PLAN VERSUS HUMAN WILL

That's what was happening by the time we reach the day when everything changed, and I don't mean a change in Joseph's life. I mean a change in the entire direction of human history.

Jacob sent Joseph to check on his brothers and the herds. When the brothers saw Joseph in the distance, their blood boiled. They began to plot Joseph's murder even as he walked toward them. They said to one another, "Here comes this dreamer! Now then, come and let us kill him and throw him into one of the pits; and we will say, 'A wild beast devoured him.' Then let us see what will become of his dreams!"

In a 1947 article on story writing, C.S. Lewis wrote, "Free will is the *modus operandi* of destiny."[1] He was referring to stories that begin by prophesying a future event. Someone in the story decides to stop the prophecy from being fulfilled. Their action to keep the prophecy at bay then becomes the catalyst that brings the prophecy into reality.

God creates a plan, then executes that plan. Does human free will get in His way? No. He uses our free will like a painter uses a brush or a writer uses a pen.

Joseph's brothers reasoned that by killing him, they would make it impossible for God to fulfill their brother's prophetic dreams. Then a more lucrative opportunity presented itself. They saw a caravan of Ishmaelite traders headed for Egypt. They sold Joseph to them. This would allow them to rid themselves of their brother and make a little money on the side.

They sold their brother to their distant relatives, the Ishmaelites, dipped his coat of many colors in goat's blood, and took it back to their father. They convinced Jacob that a wild animal had devoured his favorite son.

As a teen, Joseph was sold into bondage. (Today we would call this human trafficking.) He became an alien in a distant land where people spoke a strange tongue. In Egypt, the Ishmaelites sold Joseph to a man named Potiphar.

Even while in slavery, Joseph lived by God's rules. He worked hard. He was honest. He was reliable. God gave him wisdom and understanding. Joseph became extremely valuable to Potiphar. He moved up quickly through the ranks. He was still a slave, but he soon came to be second in command of all of Potiphar's estate.

Even as a slave, Joseph found biblical success. Genesis 39:2 says, "The LORD was with Joseph, so he became a successful man." With Joseph in charge, Potiphar's estate flourished. God's blessing on Joseph became a blessing over all Potiphar's domain (verse 5).

POTIPHAR'S TROPHY WIFE

As the years passed, Joseph grew into a handsome young man (Genesis 39:6). Potiphar's wife noticed. Genesis 39:7 says, "His master's wife looked with desire at Joseph, and she said, 'Lie with me.'"

The Bible tells us little about Potiphar's wife. However, we can speculate with some confidence. In that day, men with rank, power, and wealth often had whole harems. Their wives were the most beautiful of the land. Today, we might call Potiphar's wife a trophy wife. Everything about her would have been enticing—her hair, her smile, her voice, her clothing, her perfume, her figure. And she was on the hunt for Joseph.

At this point in history, the Ten Commandments remained hundreds of years in the future. But Joseph walked with God. He knew right from wrong. God had not yet carved "Thou shalt not commit adultery" into stone tablets, but He had written it on Joseph's heart.

Joseph adamantly refused the woman's advances. He explained that to lie with her would betray the confidence of his master and would be a sin against God. She persisted. She made the seduction of Joseph the goal of her life. The Bible says that Joseph ran Potiphar's estate so well that Potiphar's big concern became what to order for his next meal. His wife also would have had lots of time on her hands. She had time for a hobby, which became Joseph.

One day, the course of Joseph's duties brought him into the house. He suddenly found himself alone with Potiphar's wife. Genesis 39:12 says, "She caught him by his garment, saying, 'Lie with me!' And he left his garment in her hand and fled."

She cried rape. She told the other servants that Joseph tried to force himself on her. She appealed to their prejudice against Hebrews. "See, he has brought in a Hebrew to us to make sport of us; he came in to me to lie with me, and I screamed. When he heard that I raised my voice and screamed, he left his garment beside me and fled and went outside" (verses 14-15).

When Potiphar came home, she told him a similar story, and Potiphar's "anger burned" (verse 19). Despite his initial anger, we have good reason to believe that Potiphar guessed who the real culprit was. It was a capital offense for a slave in Egypt to force himself on his master's wife, but Potiphar did not have Joseph executed. As captain of Pharaoh's bodyguard, Potiphar had Joseph thrown into a special prison reserved for the king's prisoners. This was no country club. It was the kind of place where Pharaoh would want his enemies to suffer. Joseph called it a dungeon (Genesis 40:15).

JAILHOUSE PROSPERITY

Joseph's focus on pleasing God made him his father's favorite son. This got Joseph sold into slavery. His focused ambition caused him to rise, even as a slave, so that he soon ran Potiphar's entire estate. Then he was falsely accused and unjustly thrown into prison. Even there, Joseph's ambition did not change and neither did his focus.

Joseph again rose quickly to a position of trust. Genesis 39:21-23 says,

> The LORD was with Joseph and extended kindness to him, and gave him favor in the sight of the chief jailer. The chief jailer committed to Joseph's charge all the prisoners who were in the jail; so that whatever was done there, he was responsible for it. The chief jailer did not supervise

anything under Joseph's charge because the LORD was
with him; and whatever he did, the LORD made to prosper.

Joseph may have thought, *Here we go again. When will the next
hammer fall?*

He could not know that the most staggering setbacks were over.
He would spend more years in prison, and he would experience other
disappointments. But from here onward, his rise would be unimpeded. In the gloom of the moment, any progress Joseph made probably felt painfully slow. Even so, he would become the second most powerful man in the world by age 30.

God had laid out for Joseph a path to honor and global consequence. Every seeming setback was a step toward receiving Pharoah's favor and fulfilling a world-saving destiny. God ordained Joseph to be the rescuer of his family and of many people throughout the known world. That sovereign path ran straight through a terrible dungeon.

Faithfulness in all kinds of seemingly small things became the key that opened the door to future triumph. Feed the prisoners, train the staff, please the warden, and keep everything as clean as possible. Dirty work. Thankless work. But Joseph did it faithfully. Focused ambition made Joseph so trustworthy that the head of the prison put increasingly more important jobs in Joseph's hands.

PALACE DREAMERS

One day, two men of note arrived at the jail—Pharaoh's chief cupbearer and chief baker. The captain of the guard knew that Pharaoh sometimes changed his mind about imprisoning high officials. Today's prisoner might be restored to power a few days later. So, he put his best man—Joseph—in charge of them.

One night, both the cupbearer and baker experienced strange dreams. Joseph interpreted those dreams for them. After all he had gone through, he still believed that God would fulfill the dreams he had experienced as a child.

The baker's dream communicated bad news. Joseph had to tell him that he would be sentenced to death and hanged within three days. But the cupbearer's dream revealed that he would be set free and restored to his office, also in three days. Joseph entreated the cupbearer to remember him when he stood before Pharaoh after his release.

Joseph's interpretations proved perfectly accurate. But the cupbearer forgot his promise to tell the king about Joseph and the injustice of his dilemma. We don't know how Joseph felt as he continued to labor in prison, seemingly forgotten.

Two more years passed. Now 30, Joseph had spent half his life in servitude. Did he doubt God? Did he question God's fairness? We can guess that he had bad days. Yet we know that he remained close to God and continued to focus his ambition on pleasing God. We know this because the opportunity of a lifetime was about to come, and it required Joseph's continued closeness and unimpeded access to God.

PHARAOH'S DREAMS

One night, a dream awakened Pharaoh. The Bible gives specific details about that dream and what happened next. From those two things, we can surmise what went through his head when he awoke. He probably thought, *Hmm. Weird.* Then, like most adults who experience a bad dream, Pharaoh rolled over and went back to sleep.

He then had another dream—like the first, but even weirder. The next morning, the dreams were still on his mind. They troubled him. He called upon all the magicians and wise men of his court, but no one could interpret the dreams.

At that point, the cupbearer remembered his prison dream and the man who interpreted it. He told Pharaoh the whole story. Pharaoh commanded that Joseph be brought before him. They hustled Joseph out of the prison. He cleaned up, shaved, and changed his clothes.

Pharaoh told Joseph the dreams and that he had heard Joseph could interpret dreams. Joseph explained, "It is beyond my power to do this…but God can tell you what it means and set you at ease" (Genesis 41:16 NLT).

Joseph began by giving credit to God. Focused ambition will properly order your priorities. It will give you the perfect combination of confidence and humility.

You can read about the dream and Joseph's interpretation of it in Genesis 41. The important point here is that Egypt was about to have seven years of plenty, then go into a period of severe drought and have seven lean years. The lean years would swallow up the prosperity that went before them.

After interpreting the dream, Joseph advised Pharaoh,

> Now let Pharaoh look for a man discerning and wise, and set him over the land of Egypt…let him exact [20 percent] of the produce of the land of Egypt in the seven years of abundance. Then let them gather all the food of these good years that are coming…Let the food become as a reserve for the land for the seven years of famine which will occur in the land of Egypt, so that the land will not perish during the famine (Genesis 41:33-36).

God gave Joseph favor with Pharaoh and his advisors. They believed Joseph's interpretation of the dreams. More than that, they saw the wisdom of his advice on how to prepare for the bad years. Pharaoh, greatly impressed, put Joseph in charge of the entire operation. In a matter of hours, he went from imprisoned Hebrew slave to the second most powerful person in the greatest nation on earth.

RESCUING ISRAEL AND THE WORLD

The next 14 years all happened exactly as Joseph had said. During the seven years of abundance, he stored food in cities across Egypt. Then came the lean years. Famine broke out, but not just in Egypt. Genesis 41:57 says, "People of all the earth came to Egypt to buy grain from Joseph, because the famine was severe in all the earth."

The desperation of those days eventually spread to Canaan. Jacob heard that grain could be bought in Egypt, so he sent his sons there. To buy large portions of grain required that they go to the leader in charge of grain sales and distribution—Joseph. He recognized his brothers on sight. But he had been a mere boy when they last saw him, and now he stood before them as an adult in the garb of an Egyptian ruler. The brothers did not recognize him.

The details of the story are intriguing and if you don't know them, read Genesis chapters 41 through 50. I want to focus on what happened when the brothers finally figured out the identity of the man in charge of Egypt's grain sales. The high official who held their lives in his hands was Joseph, the brother they wanted to kill, but instead, sold into slavery.

They were terrified, but Joseph showed them mercy. He told them to tell his father that he was alive and to come to Egypt with his entire clan and live there. God confirmed to Jacob that he should do this. Years later, when Jacob died, the brothers felt sure Joseph would finally take his revenge on them. They bowed down at Joseph's feet and asked for mercy. In Genesis 50:20, Joseph said to them, "You meant evil against me, but God meant it for good in order to bring about this present result, to preserve many people alive."

Joseph's answer summarizes his life and stands as a lesson for any-one who makes biblical success his preeminent ambition. Obstacles and setbacks are not meant to destroy us, but to help us fulfill God's purposes in our lives. Whatever happens, we must maintain focused ambition on biblical success. That means doing the right thing even in the darkest dungeon.

The whole world needs men like Joseph. That means we need to *be* men like Joseph. Real men possess focused ambition.

STUDY QUESTIONS

1. In a world that is so full of distractions, many of us struggle with the inability to focus. On a scale of 1-10, how is your focus? (10 being the "eye of the tiger" and 1 being "ever distracted"). Where do you see room for improvement?

2. Ambition that is selfish will lead to all kinds of evil. Drive that is God-directed leads to good. In your phase of life, who do you see as driven to do evil and who is driven to do good? When it comes to your ambition, what would family and friends say about you?

3. Satan uses many different kinds of distractions to remove our focus from God. Which ones does he most often use on you? Examples: television, video games, sleep, friends, addiction to anything that makes you a slave, etc.

4. God had a great task for Joseph—to save his family and the world from hunger. In your mind, what were the three top distractions or dangers he faced along the journey?

5. What is the Holy Spirit teaching you about your life and your ambitions? Are you passionate about the right things? Are you focused on seeing them through?

6. Get focused. Get busy for Jesus. What are your next three steps?

PART 3:

REAL MEN ASSUME RESPONSIBILITY

Real men go beyond minimum obligations. They reach above the call of duty. They take responsibility for themselves and others. Jesus showed that taking responsibility often requires humility before others and in service to them.

Whoever wishes to become great among you shall be your servant, and whoever wishes to be first among you shall be your slave; just as the Son of Man did not come to be served, but to serve, and to give His life a ransom for many.

MATTHEW 20:26-28

Bear one another's burdens, and thereby fulfill the law of Christ...For each one will bear his own load.

GALATIANS 6:2, 5

The price of greatness is responsibility.[1]

WINSTON CHURCHILL

Ask not what your country can do for you, ask what you can do for your country.[2]

JOHN F. KENNEDY

8

TO DUTY
AND BEYOND

J ohn 13 begins with this profound statement about Jesus: "Having loved His own who were in the world, He loved them to the end" (verse 1). Those words lay the foundation for a period of teaching unmatched in human history. Jesus and His disciples prepared to celebrate the last Passover of the Lord's first coming. Jesus had shared other Passover meals with His disciples during their time together.

The Passover traditions were founded by God some 1,500 years earlier to show His righteous judgment of sin and His gracious deliverance to those who would believe in Him. The sins of the Canaanite nations were full; the 420 years of slavery of the Jews were coming to an end. God sent ten plagues to loosen the grip of Pharaoh. The final plague was a death angel who would kill all the firstborn males in the land of Egypt. This was a just judgment against the Egyptians. Yet the compassion of God compelled Him to provide a way of salvation. If anyone would trust in the living God and sacrifice a one-year-old unblemished lamb and place its blood on their door mantle, the death angel would "pass over" that home and the firstborn would be saved.

Yet this Passover was unique for Jesus and His disciples—as well as for every human being throughout time. Jesus was about to become the ultimate Passover Lamb. Within hours, He would die so that all who believe in Him would have life and freedom.

The teaching begins in John 13:3:

> Jesus, knowing that the Father had given all things into His hands, and that He had come forth from God and was going back to God, got up from supper, and laid aside His garments; and taking a towel, He girded Himself. Then He poured water into the basin, and began to wash the disciples' feet and to wipe them with the towel with which He was girded (verses 3-5).

GOD IN SERVICE

Jesus knew who He was—He knew His eternal position as the second person of the Trinity, God the Son. He knew that God the Father had placed everything in His hands, that He had come from God and would soon go to God. In the same sentence as those astounding statements, John described Jesus getting up from the table, removing His outer garments, picking up a towel, and tying it around His waist. He poured water into a basin, then went from disciple to disciple, kneeling before each one to wash his feet, and wiping them with the towel around His waist.

The Gospel of John describes this scene with an amazing economy of words, so it's easy to read right past it. Don't do that. Look carefully at the words inspired by the Holy Spirit to describe this extraordinary moment in the history of the universe. God became man and humbled Himself. God became man, born of a simple virgin in a stable, His first crib a feed bin. God became man, took off

His outer garments, took a towel, and tied it around His waist. God became man, picked up a basin, and knelt before each disciple. God in human flesh took on the job, attire, and attitude of a slave. Love poured through His being and expressed itself as service.

> Have this attitude in yourselves which was also in Christ Jesus, who, although He existed in the form of God, did not regard equality with God a thing to be grasped, but emptied Himself, taking the form of a bond-servant, and being made in the likeness of men. Being found in appearance as a man, He humbled Himself by becoming obedient to the point of death, even death on a cross (Philippians 2:5-8).

We would find it bizarre to join friends for a holiday meal and have someone go around washing everyone's feet. But in those days, washing a person's feet was a matter of hygiene, comfort, and hospitality. On that night, it became far more. With Jesus, it became a picture of holiness, humility, power, and love.

All of this was way too much for one disciple.

> Peter said to Him, "Never shall You wash my feet!" Jesus answered him, "If I do not wash you, you have no part with Me." Simon Peter said to Him, "Lord, not only my feet, but also my hands and my head." Jesus said to him, "He who has bathed needs only to wash his feet, but is completely clean; and you are clean, but not all of you" (John 13:8-10).

LET THIS MIND BE IN YOU

Jesus washed the disciples' feet, put His outer garments back on, then reclined at the table. He asked, "Do you know what I have done to you? You call Me Teacher and Lord; and you are right, for so I am. If I then, the Lord and the Teacher, washed your feet, you also ought to wash one another's feet. For I gave you an example that you also should do as I did to you" (verses 12-15).

What an intriguing exhortation—"Wash one another's feet"!

The Creator Himself put the towel around His waist, carried the basin of water, knelt before each of them, and washed their feet. Then He told them to serve one another. A moment later, He gave a principle we must always remember: "If you know these things, you are blessed if you do them" (verse 17). The blessing comes in the doing!

Ministers and teachers sometimes tell us to stop and let God do everything. "Let go and let God" can be great advice, or it can give people the wrong idea. When a doctor takes a biopsy, you have no control over the outcome. That's when you pray, then you "let go and let God." But when Jesus exhorts us to serve one another, He does not say, "Sit back and let God do it." He tells us to do it.

We cannot save ourselves from our sin no matter how hard we try. On our own, we cannot reach the level of righteousness God requires for heaven. We must leave that in God's hands. But salvation in Christ is not the end. It is the beginning.

Ephesians 2:10 says, "We are God's masterpiece. He has created us anew in Christ Jesus, so we can do the good things he planned for us long ago" (NLT). Our works, then, do not save us. Salvation occurs when God creates us "anew in Christ" by His grace through faith alone in Jesus. However, one of the benefits of being made new is that it opens the door for us to "do the good things he planned for us long ago."

ASSUME RESPONSIBILITY

In the foot-washing passage, Jesus did not sit at the table and complain. He did not say, "Hey, no one took care of the foot washing when we came in. Someone should do something about this." He did not pull out His smartphone and announce on Facebook: "Problem in the upper room! No one washed the disciples' feet. Someone needs to do something about this!" Neither did He just take care of His own feet. Jesus washed everyone's feet!

Jesus assumed responsibility for a task usually left to the lowest of servants. His greatness did not prevent Him from carrying out a lowly task. His greatness expressed itself in servanthood.

Real men do not run from responsibility; real men assume responsibility.

THE MAN WHO RESCUED A WOMAN AND CHANGED A NATION

The book of Ruth begins with a series of tragedies. A famine struck the land of Israel. In Bethlehem, a man named Elimelech gave up on Israel. He moved his wife, Naomi, and their two sons about 50 miles away to the land of Moab, just east of the Dead Sea.

Elimelech's choice to flee turned sour. He may have expected his stay in Moab to be brief, but he remained there the rest of his life—about ten years. After Elimelech died, his sons took Moabite women as wives. But then the sons died too.

Into this time of darkness came a glimmer of hope. Bereaved Naomi, Elimelech's wife, heard news from her homeland that "the LORD had visited His people in giving them food" (Ruth 1:6). Israel's drought had ended, and Naomi decided to return home. At first, both her daughters-in-law joined her. The three widows began the journey to Bethlehem together.

Naomi soon thought better of the situation. She felt it would be unfair to compel these young women to join her. In love, she released them of their obligations to her.

Even today in many parts of the world, when a dowry is paid for a wife, the widow needs to be released by her husband's family. Often, they demand a portion of the dowry returned. For the daughters-in-law to go to Israel with Naomi meant leaving their families, friends, traditions, and favorite places. They would live as aliens in a foreign land.

> Naomi said to her two daughters-in-law, "Go, return each of you to her mother's house. May the Lord deal kindly with you as you have dealt with the dead and with me. May the Lord grant that you may find rest, each in the house of her husband." Then she kissed them, and they lifted up their voices and wept. And they said to her, "No, but we will surely return with you to your people." But Naomi said, "Return, my daughters. Why should you go with me? Have I yet sons in my womb, that they may be your husbands? Return, my daughters!..."
>
> And they lifted up their voices and wept again; and Orpah kissed her mother-in-law, but Ruth clung to her (Ruth 1:8-12, 14).

"INTREAT ME NOT TO LEAVE THEE"

Both women clearly loved Naomi. Both wept at the thought of being separated from her. But with Ruth, something more was at work. The last phrase shows the difference: "Orpah kissed her mother-in-law, but Ruth clung to her."

Orpah turned back toward Moab as instructed. Naomi then said to Ruth, "Behold, your sister-in-law has gone back to her people and her gods; return after your sister-in-law" (verse 15).

Verses 16 and 17 tell us Ruth's response. Her words of devotion and love have brought goodwill with people ever since. Her answer was simple and majestic. I especially love how it is rendered in the King James Version:

> Ruth said, Intreat me not to leave thee, or to return from following after thee: for whither thou goest, I will go; and where thou lodgest, I will lodge: thy people shall be my people, and thy God my God: Where thou diest, I will die, and there will I be buried: the LORD do so to me, and more also, if ought but death part thee and me.

JOURNEY TO A NEW HOME

When Naomi saw Ruth's determination, she stopped urging the young woman to leave and they started for Bethlehem. Their journey was arduous. They began at an elevation of more than 2,000 feet, perhaps as high as 4,000 feet. They descended to the Dead Sea, the lowest-elevation land on earth—1,400 feet below sea level. Then from the Dead Sea to Bethlehem, they climbed back up another 4,000 feet.

In Bethlehem, Naomi owned a piece of property inherited from her husband. The property apparently produced nothing after Elimelech left. So while Naomi had some land, she arrived with nothing else. But, unlike most ancient nations, Israel's laws (given by God) made provisions for the poor.[1] One of those provisions had to do with harvest. When a farmer harvested his fields, he was to leave the corners unpicked as a provision "for the needy and for the stranger" (Leviticus 19:10).

As the two widows traveled to Bethlehem, Naomi must have told Ruth about this merciful provision in the law. When they arrived, Ruth volunteered to go and harvest grain in the fields. Naomi came home to Israel, but Ruth arrived as a foreigner. She probably did not speak the language well. To her, the people looked, ate, and talked in strange ways. She was an alien in this land. She must have felt completely out of place and vulnerable as she arrived to glean whatever crops she could.

A FIELD OF BOAZ

Ruth "happened" upon a field belonging to a man named Boaz, a relative of Elimelech. Ruth 2:1 describes him as "a man of great wealth." Under the law, she had the right to glean the leftovers from the corners. But when she approached the men working in the field, she did not demand her rights. She showed humility and courtesy. She asked the men, "Please let me glean and gather after the reapers among the sheaves" (verse 7).

While Ruth worked, Boaz showed up. Notice the atmosphere of God-centered camaraderie he created with the men who worked for him. Ruth 2:4 says, "Now behold, Boaz came from Bethlehem and said to the reapers, 'May the LORD be with you.' And they said to him, 'May the LORD bless you.'"

LIGHT IN A TIME OF DARKNESS

Ruth's family story took place during the historical period of Israel's judges, which we can describe as 300 years of civil madness. The end of the book of Judges illustrates the darkness and lawlessness of those times by telling us everyone did what was right in his own eyes. This makes Boaz and his workers' greetings even more remarkable.

It shows that even in times of moral and political chaos, God has His men—men like Boaz and those who worked for him, men who openly love the Lord.

Boaz visited the field that day and looked over the work being done. He saw this poor foreigner woman hard at work and asked the foreman of the crew about her. At the time Boaz asked, Ruth was resting, but the foreman had been keeping an eye on her. He told Boaz that she was a hard worker and had kept at it all morning before taking a break. He told Boaz, "She is the young Moabite woman who returned with Naomi from the land of Moab" (Ruth 2:6).

Naomi's return to Bethlehem had been big news in the village. Her story of Ruth staying with her rather than returning to the Moabites had apparently impressed many, including Boaz. He approached her and said, "Listen carefully, my daughter. Do not go to glean in another field; furthermore, do not go on from this one, but stay here with my maids. Let your eyes be on the field which they reap, and go after them. Indeed, I have commanded the servants not to touch you. When you are thirsty, go to the water jars and drink from what the servants draw" (verses 8-9).

In response, Ruth fell on her face, bowing to the ground. "Why have I found favor in your sight that you should take notice of me, since I am a foreigner?" (verse 10).

Boaz replied,

> All that you have done for your mother-in-law after the death of your husband has been fully reported to me, and how you left your father and your mother and the land of your birth, and came to a people that you did not previously know. May the LORD reward your work, and your wages be full from the LORD, the God of Israel, under whose wings you have come to seek refuge (verses 11-12).

Boaz greeted his workers with a blessing, and then he blessed Ruth. His blessing was twofold. He blessed her physically by providing food, water, and protection. He also prayed a marvelous prayer of blessing over her, acknowledging her as a new member of God's covenant people.

In verse 13, we read this beautiful reply from Ruth: "I have found favor in your sight, my lord, for you have comforted me and indeed have spoken kindly to your maidservant, though I am not like one of your maidservants."

Consider just how comforting Boaz's words and actions would have been. Ruth was alone. She was vulnerable to all kinds of evil. The book of Judges ended with the gang rape and murder of a concubine who happened to be from the area of Bethlehem. Ruth could have been made fun of, threatened, treated violently, or even raped and killed. Instead, the hand of God moved her to a field where the workers reflected their boss's cordiality and love of God. Then, the man in power took notice of her and spoke to her "kindly" (verse 13).

BEYOND DUTY

When men of God see a crisis or need, they go above and beyond mere duty. The law required Boaz to let Ruth glean from the corners of the field. He went beyond that. Eventually, Boaz would serve as Ruth's kinsman redeemer, a position he was not legally required to take. This involved a significant financial commitment on his part. He would buy Naomi's land and agree to care for her as well as Ruth. And he would marry Ruth.

Okay, I know what you may be thinking. Ruth was probably beautiful, and Boaz was an older guy trying to score points with this lovely young woman. Some would read this, raise an eyebrow, and ask, "What did Boaz *really* want?"

Do you know what he really wanted? The blessing of God in his life. He wanted his creator to look at his life and smile. He didn't want to merely do what was minimally expected of him. He wanted to assume responsibility.

Was Ruth beautiful? Absolutely! Everything we know about her is beautiful. Was she beautiful in appearance? We don't know. The Bible doesn't say. That's interesting because the Old Testament describes several women as having a lovely appearance.

Boaz ended up marrying Ruth, but he had not intended to find a trophy wife. He was surprised to learn that Ruth was willing to marry him instead of a younger man. A dirty old man looking only for youth and an attractive figure would have found a young Israeli woman who would fill the bill with less expense.

But in Ruth, Boaz received so much more. I have every confidence that Ruth was a magnificent wife for him. I am also confident that he was a magnificent husband to her. Yet that's not how their relationship began. It began with Ruth's devotion to her mother-in-law and Boaz's desire to please God.

WHAT THE WHOLE WORLD NEEDS

I have known dozens of people whose stories I could cite as examples of assuming responsibility. I wish I could tell you about each one. Some reach out to the elderly, some help young people prepare for work and employment, some feed and clothe the needy. They do it for Jesus and in His name. They do it out of genuine love.

Today the whole world stands in desperate need of men who do more than take care of themselves. We need men who not only fulfill their duties to others but go beyond—we need men like Boaz! America and the world are starving for men who will see a need, stand up, and assume responsibility. We need men who see their obligations as a starting point, not a finish line. Real men assume responsibility!

STUDY QUESTIONS

1. Everyone in the upper room saw the need for someone to wash their dirty feet. Jesus modeled what real men do. They see the need and act, even when the task is "below their pay grade." What do you see that needs to be done in your world? In your church? In your family? In your business? In your Bible study group?

2. How did Boaz assume responsibility for himself? Why did he allow the poor to glean and harvest in his fields? Read Ruth 2:11-12. What compelled Boaz to go above and beyond for Ruth?

3. Ask the hard questions: Do you avoid responsibility or assume it? What would your family say? What about your friends, classmates, business partners, staff?

4. When was the last time you went above and beyond for someone else for God's glory? Be honest. Where do you see room for improvement?

PART 4:

REAL MEN EXHIBIT GODLY CHARACTER

Good character matters. Its value is beyond measure. Character involves honesty, courage, righteousness, and virtue in every aspect of life. Real men reflect God's character as revealed in Scripture, and we can see how much God cares about character in the following passages:

A good name is to be more desired than great wealth, favor is better than silver and gold.
PROVERBS 22:1

Even a child makes himself known by his acts, by whether his conduct is pure and upright.
PROVERBS 20:11 (ESV)

I would rather be a little nobody, than to be an evil somebody.[1]
ABRAHAM LINCOLN

What is more valuable than gold? Diamonds. Than diamonds? Virtue.[2]
BENJAMIN FRANKLIN

10

DEVELOPING AND DEPLOYING CHARACTER

A media assault on good character has been going on for years. "Women like bad boys," is one popular saying. Another is "Good character makes you boring and predictable." In a sense, that is correct—good character does make you predictable. But I prefer a different term: Good character makes you *dependable*.

A man of bad character may come through for you, or he may not. A bad boy might stand up for you one minute, then throw you under the bus a minute later. Bad character is hit and miss. But good character means consistency and is the hallmark of trustworthiness. If a man of good character says he will do something, only the most dire, unforeseen circumstances will stop him. A man of good character will have your back every time. Today's culture may call him boring, but in reality, good character makes a man awesome!

Some people, unfortunately, do not pay enough attention to a man's character. If a man is lacking in this area, people often overlook it and say, "Give him time. Things will be okay." But it almost never works that way. A man does not change his character unless he is strongly self-motivated to pursue God and seek the character qualities God desires in his life. Apart from that, he won't change.

Never assume that you can motivate a man to improve on his character. Nor will getting married and becoming a father cause a man to change. The desire to change has to come from within, as God convicts his heart.

A man of good character will do his job and will care about the people around him. He will make a good husband and a good father. Because he realizes the importance of character, he will provide for his family the moral underpinnings and Christian worldview they need in order to make right choices that please God.

GOOD IS GOOD, BAD IS BAD

As a young Christian, I pored through the Bible every chance I got. In the book of Proverbs, I found what seemed like a secret instruction manual. That sounds absurd because it's part of the bestselling book of all time, the Bible. But Proverbs taught me principles that few people understand. The book is so relevant today that it seemed to have been written just for me and for anyone else who is willing to receive its wisdom. It tells a young man what is important and how to be the kind of man who succeeds at important things.[1]

I read Proverbs over and over. The first verse of chapter 22 stood out to me: "A good name is to be more desired than great wealth." Reputation is based on character and is far more important than title, occupation, education, or monetary wealth. The size of your 401(k) carries only transitory value. Your character matters forever. Good character does *not* qualify you for heaven. Only the righteousness of Christ can do that (2 Corinthians 5:21). But good character will reap eternal rewards (1 Corinthians 3:11-15).

In Proverbs 22:1, God calls favor "better than silver and gold." In Scripture, we find the word *favor* used in different ways, and in Proverbs 22:1, it means that if you have a good name, people will generally (though not universally) respect and honor it. Favor a good name, good character, a good reputation—these are far more important than money. Yet these qualities tend to bring financial stability and success.

The world's philosophies change, but godly character transcends time and geography. Character refers to a person's moral perspective—how he thinks, how he processes information, and what he values. Godly character results in conduct rooted in the character of God.

HOW TO DEVELOP GODLY CHARACTER

To develop godly character, go to God's Word. Proverbs 29:18 says, "Where there is no vision, the people are unrestrained." In the original Hebrew text, the word translated "vision" refers to the kind of vision received by a prophet of the living God and recorded in the Bible. Without that kind of revelation—without God's Word—the people cast off restraint.

America's second president and one of her Founding Fathers, John Adams, wrote, "We have no government armed with power capable of contending with human passions unbridled by morality and religion. Avarice, ambition, revenge and licentiousness would break the strongest cords of our Constitution, as a whale goes right through a net."[2]

If people do not respect God's revelation, they will cast off restraint. We see this all the time on the news. Sinful behavior is what happens when people lack appreciation for God and the revealed Word of God.

Without God's Word, people are unrestrained and they have no guidelines by which to measure good and evil. Imagine the length of 12 inches meaning one thing to one contractor and something different to another. Confusion would doom the structure, no matter how much money went into its construction. Similarly, without revelation from God, people are left guessing. Each person holds his own opinion of right and wrong, creating moral chaos from the entertainment world to the classroom to the government. Jesus compared such chaos to building a structure on shifting sand (Matthew 7:24-27). Without God's Word as a guide, lives are warped—they are twisted, left askew, and made unstable and unreliable.

God provided the Bible as His primary revelation to humanity. That's where we find the key to cultivating godly character. If you want good character, saturate yourself with Scripture.

STRENGTH IN THE STORM

When I start leading a new men's group, I say, "Read three to six chapters of the Bible each day. Start in the New Testament. In six months, you will not be the same person."

It's crucial that we ingest God's Word regularly because our minds are a battlefield. According to *Forbes* magazine, "Digital marketing experts estimate that most Americans are exposed to around 4,000 to 10,000 ads each day."[3] So much is competing for our attention.

Consider the techniques used by the advertising industry to influence you. First John 2:16 warns against "the lust of the flesh, the lust of the eyes, and the pride of life" (NKJV). What stands at the core of almost every advertising message you see? *The lust of the flesh, the lust of the eyes, the pride of life*, or some combination thereof. These elements are almost ubiquitous in advertising. First John 2:16 goes on to warn us that a message based on any one of these things is "not from the Father, but is from the world."

THE THREE LUSTS (DESIRES)

When John talks about the three lusts, he is warning about what Ephesians 6:12 calls "the world forces of this darkness." "The god of this world" leads those forces (2 Corinthians 4:4). His name is Satan. Jesus called him "the ruler of this world" (John 16:11). Those forces want to manipulate us with "the lust of the flesh, the lust of the eyes, and the pride of life."

Experts in thought manipulation craft most of those 4,000 to 10,000 advertising messages. They stimulate the mind in ways that tend to draw us away from God's standards. But advertising represents only part of the worldly information that daily floods our minds.

Think about what you see and hear *between* the ads—the music, scripted television shows, "reality" shows, video games, news, films, magazine articles, and on and on. More than you can even fathom, the world draws you with the three lusts and inundates you with messages contrary to God and His Word.

If you're empty, the world will attempt to fill you. But being saturated with God's Word leaves no room for Satan's influences. Your mind is a battlefield. Fill it with God's thoughts. Otherwise, the world's message will become the context for your understanding of everything, even God's Word. Turn that around. Make God's Word the context for your understanding of everything, including the world's messages.

THE BIBLE OR BUST

Second Corinthians 10:5 speaks of "taking every thought captive to the obedience of Christ." How can we do that if we don't know what Christ said? Or if we constantly feed our minds on the thoughts of Satan and the world, and ignore or mostly ignore what God tells us? More than ever before, we need to saturate ourselves in God's Word.

Suppose I asked you to name the cast of *NCIS* or *Young Sheldon*. Or if you watch older shows, the cast of *Happy Days* or the nine members of *The Brady Bunch* household. Most American Christians could do that easily.

Then suppose I asked you to name the Ten Commandments. How would you do? When surveyed, most American Christians fail miserably in naming the commandments. It is no surprise that most non-Christians can't name them, but it is shocking that so few Christians can.

That is a huge problem. Lack of Bible knowledge means lack of orientation to God. Christians who do not consciously orient themselves to the Bible tend to be oriented to Satan's world system. That's why it is becoming more and more difficult to see a difference between churches and civic or social clubs. Yet the difference should be like night and day.

Today, many Christians are moving away from Scripture. Sadly, so are many churches. If that continues, will we see greater immorality in the church? It is a spiritual law: "Where there is no revelation, the people cast off restraint; but happy is he who keeps the law" (Proverbs 29:18 NKJV).

The more we are separated from the Bible, the more our thoughts and behaviors will deteriorate. We need to pay attention to Scripture if we want to make good choices in life. But good choices begin with good character, and good character begins with what we choose to think about. That is why it is so essential to take every thought captive to the obedience of Christ (2 Corinthians 10:5)—and that happens when we saturate ourselves with God's Word.

> Blessed is the man who walks not in the counsel of the
> ungodly, nor stands in the path of sinners, nor sits in the
> seat of the scornful; but his delight is in the law of the

LORD, and in His law he meditates day and night. He shall be like a tree planted by the rivers of water, that brings forth its fruit in its season, whose leaf also shall not wither; and whatever he does shall prosper (Psalm 1:1-3 NKJV).

CHARACTER IN THE FURNACE

Character must be developed and deployed…and it will be tested. One of the most famous tests of character took place in the lives of three young men. Their original names were Hananiah, Mishael, and Azariah. We know them by the names imposed on them by their Babylonian captors: Shadrach, Meshach, and Abed-nego.

The Babylonians stole the best and brightest young men from the nations they conquered. They saw the knowledge and ability of such men in much the same way they saw their enemy's gold—as resources to plunder. In the process, they transformed young men from many cultures into servants of their empire.

Babylon gave its captives a cultural baptism by immersion. They changed their manner of dress, their language, their food, and other customs. They separated them from family. For compliance, they used a combination of "carrots and sticks"—flattery and luxury along with a well-founded fear of harsh punishment. Daniel, Shadrach, Meshach, and Abed-nego were among the handsome and well-educated foreigners that Babylon planned to exploit.

YOUNG MEN WITH CHARACTER

Like Joseph, we see how Daniel, Shadrach, Meshach, and Abed-nego excelled under extreme circumstances. Also as with Joseph, God had a plan even when all seemed lost. After Daniel's interpretation of King Nebuchadnezzar's dream in Daniel 2, the king lavished him with gifts and praise. Daniel 2:48 says, "The king promoted Daniel and gave him many great gifts, and he made him ruler over the whole province of Babylon and chief prefect over all the wise men of Babylon."

The nation of Babylon contained many provinces. The king made Daniel overseer of the province of Babylon—possibly the most sought-after job in the land. Imagine how that went over with the old guard. Making matters worse, the king made Daniel "chief prefect over all the wise men of Babylon."

No doubt, Daniel's wisdom and humility helped him in this difficult situation. Still, he was young, a foreigner, a Jew, and, to the sophisticates of Babylon, a yokel from a backwater. Imagine a kid from Hicksville, USA, going to work for Apple in Silicon Valley. They start him in the mailroom, and then—in a single day—he leaves the mailroom to become Apple's most powerful vice president. How would the other vice presidents feel?

The Hicksville kid then promotes his buddies to assist him. Shadrach, Meshach, and Abed-nego worked closely with Daniel in the administration of the great province. Daniel 3:12 tells us they were "appointed over the administration of the province of Babylon." The king put four foreign-born men in their early twenties in charge of the empire's most important province.[1]

The King's Image

King Nebuchadnezzar commissioned that a statue be built. It would rise high above the Plains of Shinar, not far from the location of the long-gone Tower of Babel. This was not a building; rather, it was a piece of art—an image. It stood 90 feet in the air (Daniel 3:1), approximately as tall as an eight-story building. Artisans overlaid the statue with gold. Sunlight made the gold blaze with a brilliant, seemingly supernatural aura. On the flatlands of Shinar, the statue would be visible and often glowing over vast distances.

The Bible calls the statue an "image." We don't know what image the statue depicted. It may have been of Nebuchadnezzar himself; we know the king had a problem with pride (Daniel 4:30). He was even proud of his humility! At Babylon's Ishtar Gate, modern archaeologists discovered an inscription he wrote. He described himself as "the untiring Governor, who...is constantly concerned with the wellbeing of Babylon...the wise, the humble...King of Babylon, am I."[2]

Whether or not the golden statue depicted Nebuchadnezzar himself, he certainly took it personally when the young Hebrew men defied his decree to bow down before it.

The King's Decree

Daniel 3:5 says that at the sound of certain musical signals, the king's subjects were to "fall down and worship the golden image that Nebuchadnezzar the king has set up." Verse 6 states the penalty for failure to comply: "Whoever does not fall down and worship shall immediately be cast into the midst of a furnace of blazing fire."

People sometimes call Shadrach, Meshach, and Abed-nego "the three Hebrew children"—*Hebrew* being the operative word. Their parents had taught them the Ten Commandments since birth. The first commandment says, "You shall have no other gods before Me" (Exodus 20:3 NKJV). The second commandment says, "You shall not make for yourself a carved image" (Exodus 20:4 NKJV).

When Shadrach, Meshach, and Abed-nego first arrived in Babylon, they and Daniel had risked their lives to stand by this principle. They were certainly not going to bow down to an idol now.

The King's Rage

The court of every potentate in history has been a place of intrigue—gossip, backstabbing, factionalism, prejudice, and treachery. If that sounds like office politics, you've got the picture. However, in King Nebuchadnezzar's court, office politics literally became a blood sport.

When these Judean upstarts refused to worship the idol, it created an opening for others in the court to attack them. Some of the Chaldeans went to the king and said, essentially, "Those Jewish guys have no respect for your image, your decree, or for you! The law says they must be cast into a furnace of fire."

Their words had the desired effect.

> Nebuchadnezzar flew into a rage and ordered that Shadrach, Meshach, and Abed-nego be brought before him. When they were brought in, Nebuchadnezzar said to them, "Is it true, Shadrach, Meshach, and Abed-nego, that you refuse to serve my gods or to worship the gold statue I have set up? I will give you one more chance to bow down and worship the statue I have made when you hear the sound of the musical instruments. But if you refuse, you will be thrown immediately into the blazing furnace. And then what god will be able to rescue you from my power?" (Daniel 3:13-15 NLT).

CONFIDENT BEFORE THE KING

The three young men gave a glorious answer—a statement of faith in God, His wisdom, and in heaven itself.

> Shadrach, Meshach, and Abed-nego replied, "O Nebuchadnezzar, we do not need to defend ourselves

before you. If we are thrown into the blazing furnace, the God whom we serve is able to save us. He will rescue us from your power, Your Majesty. But even if He doesn't, we want to make it clear to you, Your Majesty, that we will never serve your gods or worship the gold statue you have set up" (Daniel 3:16-18 NLT).

Confronted with the choice between courage and compromise, most people would be sweating bullets. *What do I do? Bow before the idol, or let them throw me into a fiery furnace? I hate to disappoint God, but won't He see this as a special case?*

We rarely make big decisions in the moment. We almost always decide them well in advance. These young men made the decision before they ever arrived in Babylon. They knew who they were in God. They thought and behaved as His children.

TO DIE IN CHRIST IS GAIN

Even when it is a hallway to heaven, no one wants to walk into a fiery furnace. Our bodies rebel at the thought. No one wants to suffer. But in the face of unthinkable pain, the three friends kept their focused ambition on biblical success. They saw their lives in the context of eternity. They exhibited godly character.

Though they lived in a time long before Christ's ministry on earth, they shared the attitude of Paul in Philippians 1:21: "For to me, to live is Christ and to die is gain."

Shadrach and his friends had complete faith in God's ability. They knew He *could* deliver them. They said with confidence, "God is able!" They also knew that He might not deliver them in this instance. They understood that they might suffer for the sake of righteousness (see 1 Peter 3:14).

They told the king that the survival of their mortal bodies was not the main point. God might grant them a miracle, or He might not. "But even if He does not," they said, "let it be known to you, O king, that we are not going to serve your gods or worship the golden image that you have set up" (Daniel 3:18).

BIG DECISIONS ARE PREDESTINED BY SMALL ONES

Godly character made the most important decision of their lives almost automatic. Character makes decisions, and it usually makes them in advance. If a single man on a date finds himself trying to decide whether he will sleep with the girl later on, he is in trouble! He should not wait until the height of temptation to make the decision. He should resolve to do what is right beforehand. That principle applies to any temptation we might face.

Each of these three young men had his character and devotion, godliness and righteousness tested in a horrific way. But the quality of each one's character made the test's outcome a foregone conclusion. And because the matter had been settled from the beginning, they remained at peace throughout the ordeal.

Most people would be terrified in such a situation. These young men were not in charge of their circumstances, but each of them was clearly in charge of himself and his reaction. Note the remarkable poise that filled their words: "O Nebuchadnezzar, we do not need to defend ourselves before you" (Daniel 3:16 NLT).

Do you hear the serenity in that statement? They didn't plead for their lives or try to persuade the king that his decree was unjust. They were not anxious. They were quietly resolved. With the decision made, their anxiety receded. The rest would be in God's hands. They would stand with God knowing that whatever the immediate outcome, He also stood with them. And that was enough!

Everyone knew about Nebuchadnezzar's temper. When his wise men could not describe the dream he experienced in Daniel 2, he ordered soldiers from the palace guard to hack them into pieces (verse 5). Here, he ordered his soldiers to heat the furnace seven times hotter than usual. He commanded them to tie up Shadrach, Meshach and Abed-nego, then cast the three Jewish men into the flaming furnace. Because the furnace had been superheated, the soldiers who threw the three men into it died from the heat.

Nebuchadnezzar stood on his viewing platform expecting to watch three grisly deaths. What he saw, instead, astonished the whole world of that day. Daniel 3:24-25 describes the scene:

> Nebuchadnezzar the king was astounded and stood up in haste; he said to his high officials, "Was it not three men we cast bound into the midst of the fire?" They replied to the king, "Certainly, O king." He said, "Look! I see four men loosed and walking about in the midst of the fire without harm, and the appearance of the fourth is like a son of the gods!"

SERVANTS OF THE MIGHTY GOD

Our response to trials should stand as a testimony to the existence, power, love, and care of Almighty God. Verse 26 tells us what happened next: "Nebuchadnezzar came near to the door of the furnace of blazing fire; he responded and said, 'Shadrach, Meshach and Abed-nego, come out, you servants of the Most High God, and come here!'"

The king believed in many gods. But in this moment, he saw that Someone stood above them all. The gods he had known were as nothing before the God of Shadrach, Meshach and Abed-nego. The testimony of these three young men reached far beyond the king. Verse

27 says, "The satraps, the prefects, the governors and the king's high officials gathered around and saw in regard to these men that the fire had no effect on the bodies of these men nor was the hair of their head singed, nor were their trousers damaged, nor had the smell of fire even come upon them."

In response, this pagan king said, "Blessed be the God of Shadrach, Meshach and Abed-nego, who has sent His angel and delivered His servants who put their trust in Him, violating the king's command, and yielded up their bodies so as not to serve or worship any god except their own God" (verse 28).

The character showed by the three friends enabled their testimony of God to reverberate around the known world! Next, King Nebuchadnezzar (in his own macabre way) made a decree that went everywhere. He said, "I make a decree that any people, nation or tongue that speaks anything offensive against the God of Shadrach, Meshach and Abed-nego shall be torn limb from limb and their houses reduced to a rubbish heap, inasmuch as there is no other god who is able to deliver in this way" (verse 29).

Nebuchadnezzar's violent zeal typified the time in which he lived. He used extreme threats to show his seriousness. The important point is that the whole world suddenly heard about the God associated with Israel "who is able to deliver" like no other. That's what character can do when empowered and informed by God's Word.

You will face tests, and your character will predetermine the outcome of those tests.

HOLLOW OR FILLED?

Tests reveal a person's inner qualities. I have a friend who found a massive tree blown over by a storm. He had been walking by that tree for years. It seemed healthy and strong. But when it was blown over, he could see that the tree was almost completely hollow. This made the tree too weak to withstand the storm.

Ask God to fill you with the strength of His character. Allow Him to saturate you with His Word. When He fills the hollow places in you with the might of His righteousness, you will stand strong against the storm. You will be a real man who exhibits godly character.

STUDY QUESTIONS

1. Is it possible to please God without godly character? Why?

2. The Ten Commandments are the bedrock of godly character. How many of the Ten Commandments can you write
   down from memory?

3. The Ten Commandments cannot save us from our sin
   (Romans 3:19). First, they show us we are sinful and need
   to trust in Jesus as our Savior (Galatians 2:20-21). Have
   you trusted in Jesus?

4. The Ten Commandments have another purpose: They give
   us God's moral compass. This enables us to know what
   godly character looks like. Which of the Ten Commandments did Shadrach, Meshach, and Abed-nego act upon?

5. When was the last time you consciously made a choice to
   act upon one of the Ten Commandments? What happened?

PART 5:

REAL MEN DEMONSTRATE CONSIDERATION

Jesus reiterated the Old Testament command to love your neighbor as yourself. He called it one of the two greatest commandments, second only to the command to love God. Consideration is the outworking of love. It's an awareness; godly men are aware of the emotional, physical, and spiritual capacity of those around them, and they strive to show deference to the needs of others in all those areas.

Remind them to be submissive to rulers and authorities, to be obedient, to be ready for every good work, to speak evil of no one, to avoid quarreling, to be gentle, and to show perfect courtesy toward all people.

TITUS 3:1-2 ESV

Do nothing from selfishness or empty conceit, but with humility of mind regard one another as more important than yourselves; do not merely look out for your own personal interests, but also for the interests of others.

PHILIPPIANS 2:3-4

Within the hearts of men, loyalty and consideration
are esteemed greater than success.[1]
BRYANT MCGILL

If no other consideration had convinced me of the value of the
Christian life, the Christ-like work which the church of all
denominations in America has done during the last 35 years for
the elevation of the black man would have made me a Christian.[2]
BOOKER T. WASHINGTON

12

CONSIDERATION AND TRUTH

T itus is an unsung hero of the Christian faith. He pursued biblical success (Titus 1:4-5), possessed focused ambition (2 Corinthians 8:16-17), assumed responsibility (2 Corinthians 8:6), exhibited
godly character (2 Corinthians 8:23),[1] and demonstrated consideration (2 Corinthians 7:6). He was one of the foremost among first-
century missionaries.

Titus excelled as one of Paul's missionary teammates. When the
two of them came to the Greek island of Crete, Paul asked Titus to
stay and serve the churches there. Part of his job was to go to the
Cretan villages and appoint leaders in each congregation.

Paul wrote his letter to Titus to help the young man understand
this oversight role. The first chapter of the book of Titus speaks of
qualifications for church leadership. The second chapter tells Titus
what he needed to emphasize in his teaching.

Chapter 2 ends with Paul telling Titus, "Let no one disregard
you" (verse 15). That does not mean Titus could be a tyrant. Instead,
it admonishes him to be bold, to be confident, and, if necessary, to
confront ungodly people who had come into the church. Even in

the face of criticism and threats, Titus must stick by what he knew to be true, right, and godly.

Titus 3 begins with the words "Remind them." Paul knew the Christians of Crete had been taught certain basic truths because he had been their teacher. But he also knew that it is easy to forget the basics. When legendary football coach Tom Landry's teams struggled, he didn't add more of the complicated schemes he was famous for developing. Instead, he led them in seemingly endless drills on the basics of American football: blocking and tackling.

That's what Paul told Titus: Help the church to remember the fundamentals.

SHOWING CONSIDERATION

In Titus 3:1-2, Paul tells his young friend, "Remind them to be subject to rulers, to authorities, to be obedient, to be ready for every good deed, to malign no one, to be peaceable, gentle, showing every consideration for all men."

"Showing every consideration" means to be thoughtful of others. The New Testament uses this Greek word 11 times, usually translating it as "gentle." When it says "to all men," the Greek text means "to all humanity." Show consideration and gentleness to everyone, male or female. Leave no one out. Followers of Jesus should be the most considerate people in the office, on the campus, in the supermarket line, or fishing at the lake. Why? Because we belong to Christ. Everything we do reflects on Him.

CONSIDERATION VERSUS TOLERANCE

Satan is the great deceiver (John 8:44). He would love to trick you and your kids into equating godly consideration with the modern definition of tolerance. But they are worlds apart.

The world bombards Christians with accusations of intolerance. Ironically, our critics often judge us by applying the label *judgmental* to us because people have become increasingly ignorant of Christian beliefs. Their knowledge is limited to the propaganda they hear from those opposed to Christianity. So as soon as they learn we are Christians—often before we ever say a word—they judge us. They pronounce us guilty of the one sin that, in their world, cannot be tolerated: intolerance. (Yes, I know. The irony is thick.)

They attack our most basic doctrines. For instance, Jesus said in John 14:6, "I am the way, and the truth, and the life; no one comes to the Father but through Me."

"Don't you know," they say, "that all roads lead to God?" As I shared Jesus with a friend, he responded, "I believe all who are sincere will go to heaven."

If that were true, how could anyone have assurance before God? How sincere is sincere enough? Our sincerity fluctuates according to our moods and circumstances. Jesus, on the other hand, gives us His word, and His word expresses His perfect character. He is utterly and always reliable.

Why are so many people violently angry with Christians? Why don't they just amicably disagree? Wouldn't that be an example of their highest ideal—tolerance? Instead, they try to make Christians (especially younger ones) feel guilty. They teach younger Christians, in many subtle and not-so-subtle ways, that adhering to the words of Jesus breaks society's ultimate taboo.

LOVE, TRUTH, AND CONSIDERATION

As followers of Jesus, we should not express belligerence or malice. But we must speak truth. And the truth can hurt (Proverbs 27:6).

Jesus spoke the truth with stunning candor. In Matthew 23:27-28,

He said, "Woe to you, scribes and Pharisees, hypocrites! For you are like whitewashed tombs which on the outside appear beautiful, but inside they are full of dead men's bones and all uncleanness. So you, too, outwardly appear righteous to men, but inwardly you are full of hypocrisy and lawlessness."

Jesus used strong language to try to shake them out of their religious smugness and help them realize their need for God's grace. Jesus did not say these things to injure them, but to help them see their predicament—a problem so severe only He could rescue them from it.

As frustrating and difficult as these spiritually blind people were, Jesus loved them. In Luke 19:41-42, we read, "Now as He drew near, He saw the city [Jerusalem] and wept over it, saying, 'If you had known, even you, especially in this your day, the things that make for your peace! But now they are hidden from your eyes'" (NKJV).

Jesus wept over the people of Jerusalem—He wept for their sin and blindness to the truth. He wept for the opportunity they were throwing away, and for the pain He knew they would endure as a result. Why did He weep over people who rejected Him? Because He loved them.

That must be our attitude as well. Yes, we will tell the truth. But we will not tell it with a vindictive attitude. We will let kindness characterize us and love motivate us.

Some ask why we should ever say anything unpleasant at all when we interact with non-Christians. Doesn't love and kindness mean "live and let live"?

In a 1954 James Bond novel, Ian Fleming used a play on the words "live and let live." He titled the book *Live and Let Die*. The famous movie and iconic song came out in 1973. Ironically, Fleming's title expresses what some people seem to mean when they say, "Live and let live." They mean "Live and let die." A person headed toward disaster needs a warning. There's no love in letting a blind person walk toward an obvious danger without warning him.

Society tries to manipulate Christians into silence by crying "Intolerance!" when we speak the truth. Children can be especially vulnerable to this kind of manipulation. But we need to understand—and help our kids understand—that godly consideration is different from the live-and-let-die attitude of worldly tolerance.

MORAL RELATIVISM

Do not confuse consideration with moral relativism. We accept the fact that laws govern the movement of light and the force of gravity. Almost everyone accepts such laws as objectively true. Yet our society teaches that culture and circumstance dictate moral truth. It sees morality as fluid.

This is odd because most people recognize morality as the foundation of civilization. Above ground, a building's superstructure usually allows for a bit of flexibility. By design, tall buildings sway slightly in the wind. But even there, builders must adhere to strict limits. No buildings use rubber girders or walls of water.

Above all, a foundation must be solid. The taller the building, the greater the need for a solid foundation. Before a skyscraper goes up, builders dig down deep to the bedrock. They pour massive amounts of concrete that harden into a rocklike substance. Then they build upward. If the foundation is not firm, it doesn't matter how elegantly rendered or how perfectly engineered the rest of the building. It will not endure.

BUILD ON THE ROCK

Jesus illustrated this perfectly:

> Everyone who hears these words of Mine and acts on them,
> may be compared to a wise man who built his house on
> the rock. And the rain fell, and the floods came, and the

winds blew and slammed against that house; and yet it did not fall, for it had been founded on the rock. Everyone who hears these words of Mine and does not act on them, will be like a foolish man who built his house on the sand. The rain fell, and the floods came, and the winds blew and slammed against that house; and it fell—and great was its fall (Matthew 7:24-27).

There is a God. He created everything. And He is moral. He instilled a conscience in you and me. But the moral fashions of the times can warp our consciences. A conscience might also become seared (1 Timothy 4:2). As helpful as the conscience can be, we must remember that this sin-filled world has infected it. That means our conscience does not always act as God originally intended for it to.

Our conscience works best when it is constantly refreshed by God's presence and regularly recalibrated to His Word.

We've all thrown a ball across a field. Think about the difference between a ball in free flight and a tetherball. When you throw a tetherball, it wraps around the pole. The pole is solid, and the ball is tied to it. Morality tied to God cannot fly off and do its own thing.

If you live as if right and wrong change, you are left with a vague and insubstantial morality. Without a firm moral foundation, who can authoritatively say that Hitler and the Nazis were wrong? With a changeable morality, even that evil becomes a matter of opinion. After all, Hitler was very sincere in his beliefs, even though they were horribly wrong.

A DOGMATIC BELIEF IN THE MALLEABILITY OF TRUTH

Worldly tolerance is based on an unbending belief in the malleability of truth. It speaks of "my truth" and "your truth" as if truth itself changes according to our whims. It does not. Truth can be complicated. It can be difficult to discern. But truth is always truth.

In April of 2020, *The Daily Monitor* ran an article by Alan Tacca. He wrote, "To the intelligent believer, God makes subtle changes to his identity, his character and his values in the different historical and cultural contexts where he is worshipped."[2]

According to Tacca, "the intelligent believer" believes in a god who changes with the times. Tacca's god is "with it"! In contrast, biblical Christianity does not believe in the malleability of God, but in the *immutability* of God. Through the prophet Malachi, God spoke for Himself on the matter: "I, the LORD, do not change" (Malachi 3:16).

That reality brings solace and security to individuals and to whole societies. With excruciating results, academia and entertainment have ripped away that security from culture and from individuals. They put millions of people in the dark without even a candle to light their way.

When people say, "There is no God," they transfer to themselves the responsibility for deciding what is right and what is wrong. It is a claim to deity—a burden for which humans are not equipped. If you want proof of that, consider this. During the twentieth century, openly atheistic government regimes murdered approximately 100 million of their own people. That's moral relativism in action.

Paul admonished Titus to show "every consideration" (Titus 3:2). Truth is the ultimate consideration, the ultimate kindness. Moral relativism cannot be trusted. It blinds and misleads. Therefore, Christians reject it. We embrace "I AM THAT I AM" (Exodus 3:13-14). He is Truth (John 14:6). He does not change (Malachi 3:6).

13

THREE KINDS OF CONSIDERATION

The New Testament uses the word *consideration* in three ways—consideration in society, consideration in the church, and consideration in common.

CONSIDERATION

1. Consideration in Society

In society, consideration means a loving openness to other people. We want them to hear about Jesus, and we want to exemplify to them the lovingkindness He represents.

But our kindness does not change the nature of God or of sin. Our love for people does not rewrite God's standard of morality. We can love them without loving their ways. Consideration in society should not be used as a means of becoming more popular with those who reject God's standards. We are God's representatives on earth, and our attitude of kindness should reflect His love for people (2 Corinthians 5:20). We should show love and consideration to all.

The apostle Paul affirmed this in 1 Corinthians 9:19: "Though I am free from all men, I have made myself a slave to all, so that I may win more." Paul was a free man and not a slave. No human stood over him as master. Yet he chose a life of service to win people to Christ.

The statement "I have made myself a slave to all" may seem impossible to put into action. How can one person possibly be a slave to everyone? We do it by showing consideration—consistent consideration to every person and in every situation.

Paul then beautifully expounded on this topic, ending with these words. "I have become all things to all men, so that I may by all means save some" (verse 22).

Does this mean Paul did immoral things with immoral people? No! Just the opposite. When we join sinners in their sinful acts, we diminish our witness of the gospel. They will not turn to us for help when they see us act just like them. If I find myself sinking in quicksand, I don't turn for help to someone sinking right beside me in the same quicksand. I turn to someone who is on solid ground.

"All things to all men" refers to morally neutral matters of culture or taste. In one situation, I might preach in a coat and tie. In another, I might wear sandals and a T-shirt. I should communicate the gospel in the context of the culture I am trying to reach. That may mean abstaining from things I know are not sinful so as not to offend those who think those things are sinful. But it never means doing God's work by breaking God's rules.

2. Consideration in the Church

Churches split seemingly every day in America because Christians have not learned a simple truth: God loves variety among His people. When I say that, I'm not talking about sin. God hates sin because it insults Him and harms us. But He enjoys our differences.

His creation illustrates the point. Look at the different kinds of fish or birds or other animals—their colors, shapes, and personalities.

Look at God's prophets. When the prophets spoke God's words, they stood at the highest level of authority. Yet even as they spoke the very words of God, they remained individuals. No reader will mistake Daniel for Jeremiah, or Jonah for Isaiah. While experiencing the highest level of inspiration from God, they remained unique. They inscribed inspiration—they wrote down God-breathed words— yet they did so as themselves.

God did not steal their individuality, nor does He steal ours. He delights in uniqueness. In Him, you are more yourself than you can ever possibly be outside of Him.

Too often, however, churches split over differences in style, preferences, culture, or manner of speech. I'm not talking about sexual sin, or lying, or stealing. I'm talking about the shade of carpet or whether all the ushers must be men wearing ties.

The Bible does not prohibit every form of judgment. In fact, it sometimes requires judgment. When choosing someone for church leadership, the Bible commands us to judge his suitability for that position (1 Timothy 1:1-13; Titus 1:5-11). When someone preaches a sermon or writes a book, God requires us to judge those words against the plumb line of His Word (2 Peter 1:21; see also Isaiah 8:20; 1 Thessalonians 5:21; 2 Timothy 3:16-17). We are also to examine ourselves (1 Corinthians 11:28; 2 Corinthians 13:5), and that, too, is a form of judgment.

But the Bible clearly tells us not to judge the person who eats bacon or the one who abstains from it (Romans 14:1-4). (If you think it is better for you to eat vegetables, then eat vegetables and leave the bacon for me!) If you can eat bacon in faith, then enjoy that freedom. Just don't use your freedom to hurt someone else—someone for whom Christ died.

In Romans 14:14-15, Paul said, "I know and am convinced in the Lord Jesus that nothing is unclean in itself; but to him who thinks anything to be unclean, to him it is unclean. For if because of food your brother is hurt, you are no longer walking according to love. Do not destroy with your food him for whom Christ died."

Be considerate in the church. Give others space and grace in Jesus.

3. Consideration in Common

In the New Testament, consideration often means to be mindful of others, honor them, and recognize their needs, in big ways and small. One day as I entered a restaurant, I opened the door for a lady who was exiting. She looked at me and said, "I can open the door myself! You don't have to open it for me!"

Her words carried an unspoken but real accusation of sexism. I asked myself why I opened the door. That made me think of my grandpa. When I was a boy, he taught me that if I came to a closed door ahead of someone else, I must open it. This was not a matter of gender, but of courtesy and consideration. He was teaching me a Christian principle: *honor others*.

When I go into a restaurant with friends, I try to open the door for them. I want to honor both men and women, and show them consideration and respect. If one of them opens the door for me, I gratefully receive that as a sign of common courtesy, of consideration, toward me.

CHIVALRY

However, I will admit that I make a greater effort to open the door for a woman than for a man. That goes back to the principle of showing special honor to women.

In 2016, Alexa Mellardo wrote an article for *Elite Daily* called, "10

Of The Sexiest Things A Guy Can Do That Have Nothing To Do With Sex." Number one on her list? Chivalry. She wrote,

> Any guy who thinks chivalry is a dying art needs to get his facts straight. Girls love old fashioned chivalry, and you can slay it, guys…Literally all you have to do is act like a gentleman. Piece of cake, right? When a girl is getting to know you, your sexy appearance will be secondary to the kind of guy we sense you are. Your actions will speak louder than words and take high priority on her checklist. She's going to take notes…Opening the door for her, getting her a seat, making sure she gets home OK and holding her hand go a long way.[1]

Polls vary on whether people consider chivalry sexist, but most agree that it is dying out. A Harris Poll from 2010 makes the case. The director of the poll, Regina Corso, said, "Women are sitting in more boardrooms and at the helms of more companies today, but there is…a sense that something else may have been lost. Four in five Americans (81 percent)—and that includes men and women—say women today are treated with less chivalry than in the past."[2]

In the following decade, things got worse. Much worse. The #MeToo movement has given us a glimpse of how degrading men's behavior toward women has become.

WOMEN AND CHILDREN FIRST

In the profusion of monuments in Washington, DC, few notice the one honoring the men of the RMS *Titanic*. The inscription reads, "To the brave men who perished in the wreck of the Titanic…They gave their lives that women and children might be saved."

Three quarters of the women survived the massive vessel's sinking. Three quarters of the men died. That was not by accident. Officers intentionally made women and children the priority when loading the lifeboats. Men intentionally gave up their positions in those lifeboats. Why? Because men are protectors. (We'll look at this more deeply in chapter 14.)

What would happen in a similar situation today? Every man for himself? Survival of the fittest? Life to the physically strongest? Men and women are equal, so let them battle one another for space on lifeboats, fighting like rats to escape the sinking ship? This is not about quaint old customs but about the foundations of civilization itself.

We have a picture of modern-day chivalry—or the lack of it—in the wreck of the cruise ship *Costa Concordia*. In 2012, it hit a rock off the coast of Tuscany. The ship capsized and partially sank over the next few hours, killing 32 people. According to the liberal magazine *The Atlantic*, "Men pushed women and children out of the way to save themselves."[3]

The story quotes a woman saying, "The people that pushed their way on to the boat were then trying to tell them to shut the door, not to let any more people on the [life] boat after they had pushed their way on…We just couldn't believe it—especially the men, they were worse than the women."

When the *Titanic* sank in 1912, several prominent men went down with her, including Benjamin Guggenheim. The *Titanic* hit an iceberg, and sank 2 hours and 40 minutes later. During that time, witnesses saw Guggenheim moving from one lifeboat to another, helping women and children board. He could be heard shouting, "Women first!" After doing what they could to help, he and his valet went back to their cabins and dressed in evening clothes. Witnesses said he put a rose in one of the buttonholes of what he was wearing.

Guggenheim explained to a steward, "We've dressed up in our

best, and are prepared to go down like gentlemen." A deck officer then ordered the steward to man an oar in one of the last lifeboats. Knowing the steward would likely survive, Guggenheim asked him to pass on a message. "Tell my wife in New York that I've done my best in doing my duty."[4]

DANGER AT SEA!

In 2 Corinthians 11:26, Paul spoke of the perils he faced on his many journeys, including "dangers on the sea."

A few years after Paul wrote that letter, he faced another peril at sea. Soldiers were taking him to Rome as a prisoner of the empire. Julius, a centurion of the Augustan regiment, led the guards in charge of Paul. Remember how real men have character? Paul's high character and his consideration toward Julius helped form a bond of trust between the two men. That bond would go on to save many lives. Acts 27:3 says that when they got to Sidon, "Julius treated Paul with consideration and allowed him to go to his friends and receive care."

Julius allowed Paul to get off the ship to be with friends because he recognized Paul's character. Although Paul was a prisoner and an accused criminal, Julius trusted Paul to keep his word and return. He knew that Paul would do nothing to jeopardize his well-being as a centurion.

Later, in the city of Myra, everyone changed ships and they continued their arduous journey, fighting powerful headwinds. When they made it to a place called Fair Havens, Paul advised them to harbor there. Mediterranean weather patterns that time of year made sea voyages increasingly perilous. But they wanted to make Crete before harboring for the winter.

Not long after leaving Fair Havens, a huge storm engulfed the ship. After 14 days of fighting for survival in the storm, everyone lost hope.

Until the day was about to dawn, Paul was encouraging them all to take some food, saying, "Today is the fourteenth day that you have been constantly watching and going without eating, having taken nothing. Therefore I encourage you to take some food, for this is for your preservation, for not a hair from the head of any of you will perish." Having said this, he took bread and gave thanks to God in the presence of all, and he broke it and began to eat. All of them were encouraged and they themselves also took food (Acts 27:33-36).

Put yourself in Paul's sandals. What would you say to your prison guards if they were in mortal danger and you had been charged unjustly? The typical human response might be "Die, Roman, die!" But Paul showed Christian consideration to all. He was considerate of their well-being physically, emotionally, and spiritually. This is what I mean when I say, "Real men demonstrate consideration." Jesus calls us to this.

STUDY QUESTIONS

1. Followers of Jesus are commanded to show consideration. What does this mean?

2. How has God shown you consideration (gentleness)? Can you think of times in the New Testament where Jesus shows consideration to people others are critical of?

3. What are the differences between consideration, tolerance, and relativism? Why does this matter?

4. In each of the Scripture passages below, how was Jesus considerate? Look for physical, emotional, and spiritual consideration.

   a. Mark 1:40-45

   b. Matthew 19:13-14

   c. Luke 19:1-10

PART 6:

REAL MEN PROTECT OTHERS

Real men protect others. Our society cringes at the biological reality of differences between men and women, especially the obvious difference in physical strength. But the Bible embraces our differences as part of God's plan and purpose in all our lives.

Rescue the weak and needy; deliver them
out of the hand of the wicked.
PSALM 82:4

Learn to do good; seek justice, reprove the ruthless,
defend the orphan, plead for the widow.
ISAIAH 1:17

De Oppresso Liber
(From Oppression We Will Liberate Them)
MOTTO OF THE GREEN BERETS

The rifle itself has no moral stature, since it has no will of its
own. Naturally, it may be used by evil men for evil purposes,
but there are more good men than evil, and while the latter
cannot be persuaded to the path of righteousness by propaganda,
they can certainly be corrected by good men with rifles.[1]
JEFF COOPER

14

PROTECTOR

In January 2020, over the course of only a few hours, a rabid coyote attacked several people near Kensington, New Hampshire. Unaware of the danger, Ian O'Reilly and his family walked in those same woods. His wife carried their youngest—a two-year-old boy. The coyote snuck up behind them and launched itself at the little boy, grabbing the hood of the child's ski suit. The mother whipped the boy away from the animal, and the two parents placed themselves between their children and the mad coyote. They tried to scare it away, but it would not leave.

As the coyote circled, the parents stayed between it and their children. "We tried to de-escalate," O'Reilly explained, "because none of us wanted to have an altercation with a coyote. Unfortunately, it had no interest in doing that. It became very aggressive and started attacking us."

O'Reilly realized that to protect his family, he had to become the aggressor. He attacked the rabid animal with his bare hands. The coyote bit the man in the leg and chest, but O'Reilly finally gained control. "There was quite a bit of snow on the ground, so I shoved the face into the snow and then eventually was able [to] put my hand on its snout and expire it through suffocation. Ultimately, one hand on its windpipe and one hand on its snout did the trick."[1]

Moms and dads stand between danger and their children. When he must, Dad goes after the wild carnivore with his bare hands. It may bite him. Like Ian O'Reilly, he may have to go to the hospital for rabies shots after the battle. Or, like other dads at other times in other places, he may not survive the encounter. But he does everything possible to keep his wife and children safe.

A TRIBUTE TO JUAN

In 2019, a couple of days after Christmas, something awful happened in a city that played a key role in my life and where I once pastored—Hemet, California. Late on the night of December 27, an apartment fire started. The family's mom woke up the dad, Juan. He did not hesitate. He helped his wife, their infant child, and 11-year-old daughter to safety.

Then Juan went back in to rescue the remaining children—4-year-old daughter Janessa, 12-year-old daughter Maris, and 8-year-old son Isaac. Juan was never seen alive again, and the three children also perished.

Family members described Juan as a big kid at heart because he and his children loved to play together. But with everything on the line, Juan was all man. He gave his life trying to rescue his kids.

Officials used the occasion to warn people not to go into burning buildings, even to save loved ones. Nevertheless, a Hemet police officer admitted, "As a father myself, I think a lot of us would think about going back in."

That was an understatement. If they see any chance at all, fathers will go back in. They will face the flames. They will rescue their kids... or die trying.

God hardwired protection into men's brains and bodies. But, to everyone's loss, our culture teaches men that this is sexist and wrong. Such teaching puts both men and women in conflict with their God-created instincts. It leaves our children, wives, churches, communities, and nations vulnerable to danger and wicked people. Men as protectors is not only written in our DNA. It is also written in God's Word.

PROTECTION—IT'S NEEDED

The baseball game was great! Jera and I had taken our daughter, her husband, and sons to see the Saint Paul Saints. They loved everything about it—the hot dogs, the clapping, the cheering, and even the game. Inside the stadium, we watched out for one another, as you would expect. After the game, however, we had to be even more cautious because our walk to the car was not in a safe area. This was our first time at that field, and we had parked a bit far away from the stream of the crowds.

I took point and my son-in-law, Josh, took the rear guard. We kept the women and children between us. I checked each alley before the others crossed. All was uneventful until we saw four men sitting on a wall a half block ahead of us. We had no choice but to walk past them on the sidewalk. Their mannerisms and movements, along with the way they joked with one another, showed clear signs of being under the influence of drugs.

As we approached them, I took a position between them and our family. After Jera and the others passed me, Josh and I both took a position behind the family as the women moved toward a stoplight about 40 feet down the sidewalk. When they got to the light, the ladies prepared to cross, but the traffic would not allow. We were trapped—heavy, fast-moving traffic on one side and four threatening men behind us.

One of the men jumped off the wall and started toward us. Josh and I kept ourselves between the women and children and this man. His comments and body language were threatening. He started speaking to my grandsons and then started to move between us into the little huddle of the women and children.

I thought, *Here we go.* I watched his hands. Did he have a weapon? I yelled out, "STOP! Back off!" as I stepped toward him. That moment was tense—*extremely tense.* Seconds seemed like hours.

He backed down. His friends called him back. The light changed, and we moved across the highway. A lot of things could have happened that night, but *no one* was going to hurt the family without a serious fight. The presence of a police officer would have been nice, but that is not always possible. God commissioned Josh and me to stand as a primary line of security for our family.

Here is the principle: Those who are stronger must protect those who are weaker from wicked people.

We live in a dangerous world. Predators prey on the weak. And nothing is more dangerous than a human predator. Thieves look for easy targets. Sex traffickers look for the vulnerable. Bullies search out weaknesses and try to dominate the susceptible. The weaker your position in any circumstance, the greater your danger. That's why God created a system or layers of protection.

LAYERS OF PROTECTION

Level 1: God Himself

God protects those who are in Christ. We see it throughout Scripture:

- 2 Thessalonians 3:3—"The Lord is faithful, and He will strengthen and protect you from the evil one."

- Psalm 46:1—"God is our refuge and strength, a very present help in trouble."

- Psalm 91:1—"He who dwells in the shelter of the Most High will abide in the shadow of the Almighty."

- Psalm 41:1-2—"How blessed is he who considers the helpless; the LORD will deliver him in a day of trouble. The LORD will protect him and keep him alive."

We hear of this protection in the testimonies from brothers and sisters in Christ throughout the world and throughout history. Over and over, God personally shows up to protect His own.

Level 2: Angels

Psalm 91:11 says, "He will give His angels charge concerning you, to guard you in all your ways." Hebrews 1:14 explains, "Are they [angels] not all ministering spirits sent forth to minister for those who will inherit salvation?" (NKJV).

We see many examples of this throughout the Bible. God often sent angels to protect His people. They are His servants, and they act at His command. Think of Jesus, who was exhausted after 40 days of fasting. God sent angels to watch over Him and serve Him. Jera and I can tell you, God has sent angels to protect us in our global efforts for the gospel.

Level 3: Human Government

According to Romans 13, God created governments for our protection. He ordained governments to punish evildoers and ensure justice for all. Because governments are powerful, evil governments do great atrocities. Good governments are essential to our well-being.

Deuteronomy 16:18-20 says,

You shall appoint for yourself judges and officers in all your towns which the Lord your God is giving you, according to your tribes, and they shall judge the people with righteous judgment. You shall not distort justice; you shall not be partial, and you shall not take a bribe, for a bribe blinds the eyes of the wise and perverts the words of the righteous. Justice, and only justice, you shall pursue, that you may live and possess the land which the LORD your God is giving you.

Level 4: Church Leaders

God created church government to protect the truth and the souls of God's people. He charges elders with protecting the church from false teachers, as well as immoral and divisive people. You need a good church for your soul's protection. Titus 1:10-11 says, "There are many rebellious men, empty talkers and deceivers, especially those of the circumcision, who must be silenced because they are upsetting whole families, teaching things they should not teach for the sake of sordid gain."

Titus 3:10-11 provides another exhortation to protect the church, this time from those who are intentionally divisive. "Reject a factious man after a first and second warning, knowing that such a man is perverted and is sinning, being self-condemned."

Hebrews 13:17 explains, "Obey your leaders and submit to them, for they keep watch over your souls as those who will give an account. Let them do this with joy and not with grief, for this would be unprofitable for you."

Level 5: Men

God appoints men to protect their families and those in their circle of influence. God gave you strength for the protection of your family and not their harm. They should find comfort and safety in you. Men bear the image of God as protectors. When He made you stronger—and even when He made you more intimidating—it was to help keep others safe, especially your family.

I love the story of Ziklag, which is told in 1 Samuel 30:1-25. Returning from a mission back to the town of Ziklag, David and his men discovered that a band of Amalekites had overthrown the town, burned it with fire, and carried off their families as plunder. In the effort to restore his own family and the families under his care, David never relented. He did everything in his power to rescue them, and he succeeded. I also love the story of Abraham rescuing Lot (Genesis 14:1-16).

Men, your very presence in the home makes it safer. Studies show a young woman with a dad at home is much safer in the dating years of her life. Sons and daughters are less vulnerable to the allures of gangs, drugs, and crime.

First Peter 3:7 says, "You husbands in the same way, live with your wives in an understanding way." Most people like that. A hardcore feminist might call it "benevolently sexist." But almost everyone wants a spouse who tries to understand them. Because so many husbands struggle with that concept, it seems sensible that the Bible would emphasize it.

Then comes a comma, followed by the words "as with someone weaker."

Ouch! Does the original text of Scripture really mean "weaker" there? Yes. That is exactly what it means. Is "weaker," in this context, a sexist word? No. In other contexts, the Bible uses this same word about *all* of us. At some point or other, in some way or another, we're all weaker than something or someone. God is stronger than all. Angels are stronger than humans. Parents are stronger than small children. And generally speaking, men are physically stronger than women.

DIFFERENT BY DESIGN

Here is reality. The average woman is physically weaker than the average man. That fact offends many people, but it is still true, as verified by research. Not only do men usually have more muscle mass, they generally have a higher percentage of muscle mass compared to body weight. This fact of nature makes women more physically vulnerable than men. A woman walking across a dark parking lot alone at night almost always feels more vulnerable than a man in the same situation.

In a 2003 episode of the TV series *Smallville*, Clark Kent's friend Chloe Sullivan explains to Clark why Lana Lang decided to take karate lessons. She told Clark that because he was a tall man, he had no idea how vulnerable a woman felt while walking at night and hearing footsteps behind her.

Okay, Clark had superpowers. But Chloe thought he was just an ordinary guy. In 2003, a TV character could still say the obvious. Women are generally smaller and weaker, less combat-capable than men. According to a study in *The Journal of Applied Physiology*, the average man has 40 percent more skeletal muscle than the average woman.[2] One study showed that women's muscle fiber is not as strong as men's.[3]

Have you ever noticed that the Olympics (historically speaking) feature almost no coed sports? The ones that exist, such as equestrian events, do not rely primarily on the strength or speed of the athlete. Women sprinters do not line up with the men sprinters. Women's basketball teams do not compete against men's teams. The new transgender movement in sports has only amplified this reality.

That is not an accident, and it is not a bad thing. It just means that men and women have different bodily designs. In no way whatsoever do the differences diminish women. Genesis 1:26-27 makes it clear that God made both male and female in His own likeness.

Instead of devaluing women, the differences illustrate the wonderfully complementary roles of men and women.

I expect men to help protect my wife on the road, my daughter at church, my grandchildren at the lake. More importantly, God expects it too!

PROTECTING THE FRIEND

Jason was the schoolyard bully. I will never forget his face, red hair, freckles, and wicked mouth. Jason was a fifth grader, and he terrorized us second graders. When we saw him head our way, we knew someone would be mocked, shoved, or hit. All of us had suffered at his hands.

Several second graders tried to report him, but he seemed to always get away with his crimes. We were told, "Learn to get along with him. Jason has some issues." We looked forward to the fall season, when Jason would move on to middle school. In the meantime, we just hoped to finish the year with our teeth in place and lunch money not taken.

One warm spring day, I hopped onto the bus…and froze. Jason was pushing a girl from my class. I looked around but saw no one to help. My mind raced. *What do I do? I can't just let him hurt her!*

I dropped my bag and pushed Jason down between the bus seats, swinging for all I was worth. I knew that if he got up, I was dead meat. So, I just wailed on him. Then I heard an amazing sound— Jason crying. All of us had cried at his hands, but now he cried. I felt him stop resisting and knew he'd had enough. I backed up, with my knees knocking and little courage, and I warned him, "If you hurt her or come after any of us, I will finish this fight!"

Jason never touched her or any of us again. He went off to middle school, and we kept all our teeth.

PROTECTING THE STRANGER

Tim touched down in Entebbe, Uganda. He was leading a short-term missions team to train church leaders. The small team consisted of two teachers and three college students. Uganda was having an election, and riots were happening throughout the country.

One morning as the team headed out to meet their students, they saw a group of men beating a woman. No one else in the vicinity seemed to care what was happening to her. Moved by a God-given sense of duty, this small group of men stepped in to help this young woman. They reached her just as the assailants were picking up rocks and bricks to kill her. Tim's team ran the men off and carried the woman to a police station for safety.

Life is dangerous. We need good men—real men.

A WORD TO WOMEN

Don't remove yourself from the levels of protection God has given you. This can include the men in your life, who are a gift from God for your safety. Today's feminist agenda makes women vulnerable. If you get married, marry a man who has a heart for protecting others. Marry a man who will protect you and your children. And if you are single, exercise caution, and consider male family members and friends as potential protectors. We live in an evil world. Coming under the protection of godly men is not shameful; it is wise.

Look at it this way: Why discard a major layer of protection from your life and your future?

If you ever have a son or sons, raise them to be protectors. Help them understand that it is their honor, privilege, and obligation to use their strength for good and not evil. Do not raise a bully. Raise a protector.

And honor such men.

15

PROTECTION'S FOUR COMPONENTS

There are four components of protection—spiritual, physical, emotional, and mental. The four intertwine. An assault obviously affects the victim physically. It also impacts the person mentally, emotionally, and spiritually. While the physical wounds usually heal, the mental, emotional, and spiritual aspects of the assault do not as easily relinquish their hold. Sometimes they even return to haunt the victim's physical health.

SPIRITUAL PROTECTION

Real men protect others spiritually. When Satan appeared in the garden in Genesis 3, he was seeking to destroy man's relationship with God. He approached Eve. He lied to her and deceived her. The Bible says God had equipped Adam to protect her, but his passivity led to the fall and destruction of this world. If only Adam had offered spiritual protection at that moment.

Satan, the world, and the flesh are assaulting us continually. God has created you to protect. Spiritually passive men open the door for their family and those they love to be harmed and destroyed by sin. It was in the local church where I first found men who weren't passive from a spiritual standpoint.

After I trusted Christ as my Savior, it was the pastors, the staff, and other men in the church who demonstrated godly living. They warned me about the lies of the devil. They shared with me the use of faith and Scripture in spiritual battles with temptations. They taught me to defend myself by using the Bible against the schemes of the evil one. It was these men who shared their victories and losses with me. Like a new Army recruit, you need a sergeant to lead you.

You may be reading this right now and feeling completely out of your league. Maybe you don't feel equipped to provide spiritual protection for anyone, much less your children, family, or others. The answer is simple: Start training today! Get rooted in a healthy church today. Plant yourself in the Bible every day. God wants you prepared for battle. Get fit so you can fight the good fight (1 Timothy 6:12). Protect others, and protect their souls.

EMOTIONAL AND MENTAL PROTECTION

Be prepared to interject yourself on behalf of others. When our daughter was little, I would tell her that someday a boy would want to take her on a date. I would ask, "What will you say to that boy?" She would respond with, "You have to ask my dad."

I started when she was small. I explained to her why this was important. "Some boys will have bad motives, and I'll be the bad guy for you. You don't have to say, 'No way!' Just say, 'Talk to my dad.'"

When she was six, people laughed at us. When she was 15, people stopped laughing. She would say, "Hey, Dad, this boy is going to be calling you. Tell him no."

I was teaching my daughter the life-altering nature of dating relationships. I was also teaching her that, as her dad, I would protect her emotionally as much as possible. Young people have emotions when dating, right? Strong ones! I would not be able to live her life for her. But I could give considerable protection with the simple rule "Ask my dad."

PROTECTION

The extrabiblical feminist movement has made women and children vulnerable. It has propagated passive men. I say this tongue in cheek, but it illustrates my point: A man hears a bump in the night and rolls over and says to his wife, "Wonder Woman, it's your turn. Go down and check it out. Don't forget the shotgun. See what you find and let me know."

Jera and I love to hike in the mountains. We often go way back in the wilderness, places with no cell signal for calling 9-1-1. And even if we somehow were able to make contact, it could take an hour or more for help to arrive.

Today, any wilderness area may have drug smugglers (and worse) on the prowl. Jera knows that in a dangerous situation, I move forward, and she moves back to a secure position. We have a whole series of steps in place. You might think this kind of advance preparation is crazy, but it's not. I have had friends who died in mountains where Jera and I had hiked. Being prepared is not crazy. It's protecting my wife.

If you are a single woman reading this, don't marry a passive man. God made men to be protectors because we live in an evil world. It's not an insult to be protected. God Himself protects us every day. He appointed governments to protect nations from evil. He created men with the instincts and strength to be able to protect their families from evil. And He calls parents to protect children from evil. Real men are part of God's plan for people's protection.

16

RESPONDING TO INJUSTICE

In Matthew 26, we find Jesus in Bethany, a village on the Mount of Olives just outside Jerusalem. Lazarus lived there, and it's the place where Jesus raised him from the dead. Jesus knew His earthly sojourn would soon end. He also knew what that meant—that He would soon die a terrible death for the sins of the world. He and His friends visited the home of a man called Simon the leper.

Matthew 26:6-7 says, "Now when Jesus was in Bethany, at the home of Simon the leper, a woman came to Him with an alabaster vial of very costly perfume, and she poured it on His head as He reclined at the table."

The Gospel of John identifies the woman as Mary, one of Lazarus's sisters. She expressed her thankfulness for the Lord's lovingkindness toward her and her family by pouring perfume on His head. Upon seeing this, the disciples became indignant: "Why this waste?" (verse 8).

John's Gospel names Judas Iscariot as the one who stirred up the other disciples. Judas said, "Why was this perfume not sold for three hundred denarii and given to poor people?" (John 12:5). Judas had an ulterior motive. Verse 6 explains, "He said this, not because he was concerned about the poor, but because he was a thief, and as he had the money box, he used to pilfer what was put into it."

Despite Judas's bad motive, his reasoning seemed sound. The disciples who joined him probably expected Jesus to approve of their righteous indignation. After all, they knew how much Jesus loved the poor.

Judas estimated the perfume's value at 300 denarii. That equaled a year's wages for the average worker of that time and place. Judas saw this as a potential windfall for his own pocketbook. To the others, the woman pouring out such expensive perfume in one flourish of affection and honor must have seemed like stuffing hundred-dollar bills into a shredder.

EXPRESS AN EXTRAVAGANT LOVE

Imagine this scene from the woman's point of view. How do you think she felt? Public expressions of love always run the risk of making us look foolish. The flow of exquisite oil expressed her love for the Lord. But the outcry against her may have caused her to think she had not been considerate of the poor. Her motive was to honor Jesus the best way she could. When a chorus of male voices rose against her, she must have felt reckless and wasteful—her embarrassment overwhelming. Perhaps she began to cry.

Jesus did not sit passively and allow this to happen. Some might say, "She had her own voice. She didn't need a man to defend her. Let her take care of herself." But Jesus stood up for her. He stood up against them all. He said, "Why do you bother the woman?" (Matthew 26:10). Can you hear His inflection? "Why are you harassing Mary?"

These are real people. This really happened. Mary did something profoundly beautiful—more beautiful than even she could understand. And the disciples had made her feel stupid and frivolous.

Jesus said,

Why do you bother the woman? For she has done a good deed to Me. For you always have the poor with you; but you do not always have Me. For when she poured this perfume on My body, she did it to prepare Me for burial. Truly I say to you, wherever this gospel is preached in the whole world, what this woman has done will also be spoken of in memory of her (Matthew 26:10-13).

Jesus would soon pour out His own life. Through the veins of His body flowed the blood of the new covenant (Matthew 26:28)—blood that would purchase salvation (Acts 20:28) for all who believe (John 3:18). This was momentous beyond imagining, eternity multiplied by the millions who would receive the salvation made possible by His sacrifice. His death—the turning point of time—was only days away. He explained that she was preparing His body for burial.

Jesus said people would remember Mary's action that day wherever the gospel was preached. Here I am in Minnesota, some 2,000 years later. That's about as far from Bethany, Israel, as you can get! And I'm remembering this woman with affection and admiration because of what Jesus did and said that day. Jesus, the perfect man—the real man—protected Mary spiritually, emotionally, and mentally that day.

DO JUSTICE

Jesus stood up for the outnumbered and harassed on other occasions as well. We must follow His example. Suppose you see someone weaker being hurt or in danger of being hurt. If you have the strength to intervene, do it. If it's a woman, you are not patronizing her to intervene on her behalf. You are honoring her. And you are honoring Jesus, no matter what her response.

Proverbs 31:9 gives us the instructions of a mother to a son who

was going to become king. She said, "Open your mouth, judge righteously, and defend the rights of the afflicted and needy." How does
a godly man respond to injustice? He judges righteously and inter-
venes wisely. Truth matters to him. Righteousness matters.

The poor are a constant in human history. In ancient times, nations
did not have social safety nets. In the Bible we find the earliest examples of laws that include rights and provision for the poor. Today in
America, "we the people" provide many benefits to the needy. But
the poor still need champions. People too often use them and their
needs for political purposes. Sadly, many of today's programs perpet-
uate the poverty they are supposed to eliminate.

Micah 6:8 says, "He has told you, O man, what is good; and
what does the LORD require of you but to do justice, to love kindness, and to walk humbly with your God?" The passage does not say
to *talk* justice, but to *do* justice. That means to do what is just. Look
out for the needy and the broken among those under your influence, and beyond.

The motivation should be clear: It's love. In John 13:34, Jesus said,
"A new commandment I give to you, that you love one another, even
as I have loved you, that you also love one another." Later that evening,
Jesus said, "Greater love has no one than this, that one lay down his
life for his friends" (John 15:13). First John 3:16 says Jesus "laid down
His life for us; and we ought to lay down our lives for the brethren."

Even at the cost of your own life, protect others. Fight the coyote! Fight him barehanded if you must. You can show no greater love.
Jesus dying on the cross for us became the ultimate example of this
truth. But such love has also been seen on battlefields, in classrooms,
at job sites, in homes, and in all kinds of other places throughout history. Remember Juan. Most of all, look at Jesus. Look at His sacrifice, His care, and His protection. Work that backward, and you can
see the kind of man you are supposed to be. Real men protect others.

STUDY QUESTIONS

1. Why do we all need protection? Just how safe is the real world?

2. What are the layers of protection God created for each of us? What happens when we deny, remove, or alter these layers?

3. Who has God placed around you to be a level of protection for you? Who has God called you to protect?

4. What levels of security do you need to have in place for you and your family? Have you thought that through? Have you made contingency plans?

5. Are people safer in your presence? Why or why not?

REAL MEN WORK WITH DILIGENCE

God works. And He made work a fundamental part of being human. Sin brought a curse on it, making work difficult and often frustrating. But it remains crucial for our psychological, physical, and spiritual well-being. God's Word exhorts us to perform our work in a manner worthy of our Savior. Real men work diligently to meet the needs of their family, advance the gospel and the church, meet the pressing needs of others, and display Jesus to others in the community.

We urge you, brethren, to excel still more, and to make it your ambition to lead a quiet life and attend to your own business and work with your hands, just as we commanded you, so that you will behave properly toward outsiders and not be in any need.

1 THESSALONIANS 4:10-12

Poor is he who works with a negligent hand, but the hand of the diligent makes rich.

PROVERBS 10:4

Hard work beats talent if talent doesn't work hard.[1]

TIM NOTKE, BASKETBALL COACH

A dream does not become reality through magic; it takes sweat, determination, and hard work.[2]

COLIN POWELL, FORMER US DEFENSE SECRETARY

17

TO STAND
BEFORE KINGS

Several years ago, a guy named Tom came to a church service with his wife and their kids. God was working in their lives. Tom knew little about Jesus or the Bible. He had grown up in a badly broken family, and he could see the damage his past training or lack of training was inflicting on his family.

Jera and I met with Tom and his wife after the service. We shared the gospel with them and told them that because Jesus Christ came into the world and died for our sins, we can become new creations in Him. They ended up trusting Christ, and God did a great work in their lives.

WHAT DOES JESUS WANT ME TO DO?

Tom had started and built a very successful business. He eventually sold it to a larger company in the industry. With the sale, Tom made a contractual agreement to work for them for one year. They would give him a down payment and pay the balance throughout the year.

One Wednesday morning, Tom came into my office ready to explode. He is a mountain of a man, and you would not want to pick a fight with him. With rage in his voice, he said, "I can't believe it! The man I sold my business to is ripping me off, Mark!" He then pounded the table and added, "Where I grew up, when somebody rips you off, you rip his head off."

Tom looked ready to do it. He was steaming mad. But then he asked the right question: "What does Jesus want me to do?" Starting with that great question, I began showing him some pertinent Scripture passages. Our discussion turned into a Bible study. Work matters to God, and His Word has a lot to say about how to follow Jesus in the workplace.

Over a lifetime, the average American will spend more than 90,000 hours on the job. That number does not include household work, church ministry, or charitable service. It doesn't include fixing meals, washing dishes, doing laundry, vacuuming carpets, moving, helping your friends move, or any of the hundreds of actions we do regularly without monetary compensation. The 90,000 hours only includes time on the job. Put it all together, and work becomes a huge part of life.

Tom's new boss was unreasonable, unjust, and even crooked. I told Tom that Jesus tells us to pray for our enemies. We looked together at several Scripture passages. We met again the next week. Tom asked if he could bring some friends the next time. Soon, we had a roomful of men.

All of us agreed to meet regularly. The group prayed weekly for Tom's boss. They prayed for each other. Members of the group worked in a variety of capacities. Over time, each one began to find new ways to submit his work life to God and commit to doing work God's way. God did amazing things through Tom's brokenness and humility.

THE SECRET OF SUCCESS IS NO SECRET

Jesus wants to radically transform our entire lives, including our work lives. We all tend to get lazy in one area or another. That's why God gave us dozens and dozens of verses on work and diligence. Proverbs 10:4 says, "Poor is he who works with a negligent hand, but the hand of the diligent makes rich."

The secret of success is no secret. It's right here: Be diligent! Lazy or undisciplined people don't get ahead. We live in a generation that says, "Everybody owes me." That attitude condemns untold millions to poverty. Do you want success? Don't wait for someone to "discover" you and make you successful. Look for work opportunities. Work makes wealth and brings honor.

Proverbs 22:29 asks, "Do you see a man skilled in his work? He will stand before kings."

Hone your skills. Don't be satisfied with "good enough." Reach higher. Stand taller. If you do, then like Joseph, you will be unstoppable. Everyone faces adversity. Circumstances will knock you down. But stay diligent and keep honing those skills. Like Joseph, you will soon rise back up the food chain of influence and productivity. The world stands in desperate need of such men.

Our youngest son, Ron, had finished Bible college and just returned home from a six-month ministry in Africa. He was hired by a great oil company in Grand Junction, Colorado. He worked his way up in positions of responsibility by applying Proverbs 10:4: "Poor is he who works with a negligent hand, but the hand of the diligent makes rich."

I often spent time with Ron's foreman, Jim, hunting in the mountains. After about six months on the job, Jim said that Ron was the most trusted man he had on the crew. Not bad for a 21-year-old! A few months later, the owner of the company called me: "Mark, it's Allen…I wish you had some more sons for me to hire. Ron is exceptional." While I appreciated the compliment, the credit was not mine. It was Ron's. He had applied the principle of diligence.

Remember Malcolm Gladwell's 10,000-Hour Rule. Work at it. Be diligent. Be relentless.

GOD AND WORK

When Adam and Eve sinned, a curse fell on humanity. Theologians call it "the fall." Some people believe work is part of that curse, but it is not. Even before the fall, God commissioned humans to do work. In Genesis 1:28, He told them to

- be fruitful
- multiply
- fill the earth
- subdue it
- rule over the fish of the sea, birds of the sky, and every living thing that moves on the earth

Genesis 2:15 says, "The LORD God took the man and put him into the garden of Eden to cultivate it and keep it." That's work.

Several of God's first commands dealt with stewardship of the land—a responsibility to which God still holds us accountable. "Be fruitful and multiply" may sound more like fun than work, but it involved more than sex. It also involved raising kids. That can be fun, too, but to do it well takes strategy and diligence. Being fruitful became painful for Adam and Eve (especially Eve) because of the fall. But work predated Adam and Eve's sin.

Work is not a curse; it is a privilege. Eden was a place of work and so is heaven.

However, the curse did change the nature of work. Genesis 3:17-19 tells what happened:

> To Adam He [God] said, "Because you have listened to the voice of your wife, and have eaten from the tree about which I commanded you, saying, 'You shall not eat from it'; cursed is the ground because of you; in toil you will eat of it all the days of your life. Both thorns and thistles it shall grow for you; and you will eat the plants of the field; by the sweat of your face you will eat bread."

Cultivating the garden of Eden was a breeze compared to the cultivation of crops in a sin-infested world. After the curse, weeds started growing. The ground refused to cooperate as fully. Work became much more difficult. Failure became humanity's new companion.

But when we take the right attitude—for instance, when we make work an act of worship—we find amazing remnants of the old joy and satisfaction. The experience of work can be blessed. It can take us from the mundane to the sublime, and in it, we can realize our purpose in our generation.

WORK IS AN ACT OF WORSHIP

Colossians 3:22-24 says,

> Slaves, in all things obey those who are your masters on earth, not with external service, as those who merely

please men, but with sincerity of heart, fearing the Lord. Whatever you do, do your work heartily, as for the Lord rather than for men, knowing that from the Lord you will receive the reward of the inheritance. It is the Lord Christ whom you serve.

We should pay special attention to four key words in this passage: "obey," "sincerity," "heartily," and "serve." Colossians 3:22 is addressed to "slaves." In New Testament times, the middle class as we know it did not exist. Most Romans were either rich or poor. Slaves were the poorest of the poor, making up about 30 percent of the population.[1] Slavery was an ordinary part of life; slaves were the working class. According to a PBS series on the Roman Empire, "All slaves and their families were the property of their owners, who could sell or rent them out at any time. Their lives were harsh. Slaves were often whipped, branded, or cruelly mistreated. Their owners could also kill them for any reason, and would face no punishment."[2]

In Jesus, such class distinctions disappeared. In those days, a man's slave might also be an elder at his church. People from every tribe, tongue, and nation were coming to Jesus, as were people from every economic status. The very next chapter in Colossians begins, "Masters, grant to your slaves justice and fairness, knowing that you too have a Master in heaven" (Colossians 4:1).

Colossians 3:22 tells slaves to "obey." That's a strong word. But let's face it: Work entails obedience. The same verse warns against "external service...merely [to] please men." It exhorts us instead to work "with sincerity of heart," knowing that ultimately, we answer to God.

Then Paul says something that can turn a loser into a winner, a failure into a success: "Whatever you do, do your work heartily, as for the Lord rather than for men, knowing that from the Lord you will receive the reward of the inheritance. It is the Lord Christ whom you serve."

From corporate presidents all the way to shift supervisors, every boss is looking for this person. If the Scripture passage above describes your approach to work, the whole world is looking for you. And they don't just need you. They are desperate for you—desperate for someone who will work with sincerity of heart and see his work as service to God.

If your work is service to God, then clearly, it matters to God. You stand for Jesus. Your work reflects Him. You don't just work perfunctorily, but heartily. You don't do just enough to get by. Instead, you go above and beyond the usual call of duty. Your job is not just a paycheck for you, but an opportunity for you to serve the Lord and reflect His beauty into the world.

The word "heartily" comes from the Greek word *psuche*. This refers to the soul. It literally means "that which breathes." To work "heartily" means to work from your innermost being. Do it "as for the Lord rather than for men...It is the Lord Christ whom you serve."

If you flip burgers for a living, do it in service to the living God. That attitude does not just lead to success; it *is* success! With this perspective, the job you once considered mundane takes on transcendent value.

Working "heartily, as for the Lord" turns a boring or ordinary job and takes it to the loftiest levels of human existence. Suddenly it is God's work, and its value will never end. "The reward of the inheritance" doesn't end with your shift, and your paycheck becomes a down payment on a reward that will never end.

Colossians 3:24 says, "It is the Lord Christ whom you serve." Don't think of yourself as a mere servant to human beings. You're not just an employee in a business. You serve Jesus!

God works supernaturally in the lives of His people. You live in this generation, at this time, and in this place for a heavenly purpose. Your life is not an accident. Everything you have gone through—your education, your work experience, your life experiences—has prepared you to be God's ambassador wherever He has placed you.

In this context, your seemingly mundane place of work then becomes a place of worship. The work itself becomes an instrument of that worship. Looking back, you see many mistakes. You sinned or you did something wrong. You should have done this or that. We all have regrets galore. But even here, Jesus is the Redeemer. He redeems your life—all of it.

You may be retired. But you're not done because God is not done with you. Your work still matters. You may be confined to a bed, but you remain His witness in your attitude, actions, and prayers for those around you.

The hours we spend working make up a big part of our lives. They are not a waste. God is not indifferent to them, so don't you be. Make your work an act of worship!

WORK IS A PLACE OF MINISTRY

The Bible study with Tom continued and grew. The group met weekly, going through Bible verses about work. Together we prayed, "God, give us courage. Help us to be better men at work. We pray for our leaders, bosses, and those whose work we direct. Help us to be men of faith and ambassadors for Jesus."

One Wednesday before our group met, my phone rang. The caller asked, "Are you Tom's pastor?"

"Yes."

"My name's Mike, and I'm his boss."

I thought, *Uh-oh*. I said, "How can I help you?"

He said, "I don't know what you're teaching him, but he's a different guy. He used to hate me. I think God is doing something. Could I come to the Bible study today?"

I said, "Mike, we would love to have you."

We talked a little bit more, and he said, "Mark, I have another favor to ask. Could I come early so you can teach me the stuff I missed?"

I said, "Mike, I would love for you to come. Would you like to come thirty minutes early?"

"I was thinking more like an hour early."

You should have seen the others when they walked into the Bible study and saw Mike already sitting there, his Bible open. What an amazing day when Mike trusted Christ as his Savior!

Tom's job mattered to God, and he influenced a whole group of people. He became Christ's ambassador to the man he thought was cheating him. Work can be a place of blessing, even if you have an unfair boss. With the psalmist, we should pray, "Let the favor of the Lord our God be upon us; and confirm for us the work of our hands; yes, confirm the work of our hands" (Psalm 90:17).

WORK IS GOOD

Maynard G. Krebs may have been the most famous beatnik of the late 1950s and early 1960s. He was the fictional sidekick of the fictional Dobie Gillis. Each week, a national television audience roared with laughter when Maynard, upon hearing the word *work*, would repeat it in a shrill, terrified voice. America laughed at an imaginary character to whom work was anathema.

In real life, however, a character like Maynard would either change his attitude toward work or wind up homeless or on the public dole. Either way, he would find himself working. People don't usually think about what hard work it is to survive as a homeless person. Navigating public and private charities also takes time, thought, strategy, and work. Nobody gets away without working. Work now or work later. If you work now, you will work toward thriving. If you work later, you will work just to survive.

Work is a good thing—unless you try to avoid it. Embrace it, and it will reward you in a thousand ways. Run from it, and it will hunt you down with the weapons of poverty and disgrace.

Even in heaven we will work. We will work with joy, and for the perfect boss. But we will work. And, as we just saw, that kind of meaning and beauty in work can begin here on earth.

WORK IS HARD

Work is hard because of the curse. We read in Genesis 3:17-19 that mankind will feed himself by the sweat of his brow. The curse removed easy life. Now it is hard to grow crops, grow a business, grow your assets, grow your portfolio. No one is exempt. We all tire and must push through fatigue. The fall made work more difficult, but work is still good.

Americans of our time have lived in the most prosperous generation ever. We have mitigated much of the hard reality of the struggle to survive. This has occurred because our country is a constitutional republic with a free-market system and the rule of law. These systems were uniquely influenced by biblical principles. The second element is the Protestant work ethic: work hard to the end. Earlier generations would find today's levels of prosperity mind-boggling.

Have you ever had food in your refrigerator end up growing mold, requiring you to throw it away? In the rest of the world, that does not happen. A 2010 study by the US Department of Agriculture showed that Americans threw away 133 billion pounds of food that year, amounting to $161 billion worth of food.[3] Where did we throw this nourishment and money? Into landfills. According to the

US Food and Drug Administration, "Wasted food is the single largest category of material placed in municipal landfills."[4]

We have been living in a land of plenty during a time of plenty—a land and time made possible by the grace of God. But, as a nation, we have not been grateful. We changed Thanksgiving from a holiday set aside for giving thanks to God into a holiday where we thank each other. We should humble ourselves before God and thank Him for His kindness. Work is hard, but hard work pays off.

WORK IS SPIRITUAL

If you believe the premise that work is an act of worship, you might say, "Well, of course it's spiritual." But while we can use a keyboard for worship, keyboards are material, not spiritual. Work is not like a keyboard. While done in the material world, work includes a powerful spiritual component.

The church in Thessalonica included members who were lazy and lacked discipline. Paul encouraged them to remember his behavior and use it as a model:

> You yourselves know how you ought to follow our example, because we did not act in an undisciplined manner among you, nor did we eat anyone's bread without paying for it, but with labor and hardship we kept working night and day so that we would not be a burden to any of you; not because we do not have the right to this, but in order to offer ourselves as a model for you, so that you would follow our example. For even when we were with you, we used to give you this order: if anyone is not willing to work, then he is not to eat, either. For we hear that some among you are leading an undisciplined life, doing no work at all, but

acting like busybodies. Now such persons we command and exhort in the Lord Jesus Christ to work in quiet fashion and eat their own bread (2 Thessalonians 3:7-12).

"Eat [your] own bread" does not mean that if you go to someone's house for dinner, you should bring your own sourdough. It refers to living off the fruit of your own labor instead of depending on others for your sustenance. Neither does it mean you should not accept help. If you get terribly sick and others from church show up with meals for you, be thankful and eat gratefully.

These verses address laziness and lack of discipline. Those are not just economic problems, but spiritual problems. If you struggle in those areas, God can help you. If you are already an industrious, disciplined individual, God can help you keep or create the right balance between your home life and work life.

WORK IS PROVISION

Ephesians 4:28 says, "He who steals must steal no longer; but rather he must labor, performing with his own hands what is good, so that he will have something to share with one who has need." "Performing with his own hands what is good" reminds us that work is good, not evil. "That he will have something to share with one who has need" shows how labor can help turn the bad citizen into a good one.

Until Jesus returns, there will be people in need. We read what Jesus said in Matthew 26:11: "You always have the poor with you." That's a sad reality. But it's also an ongoing opportunity for us to share with others.

We will not be whole and healthy if we work only toward meeting the needs of ourselves and our own families. Christians work as unto the Lord. We make our own bread and then we share that bread with others. Notice the sequence in the instruction given in Ephesians 4:28: stop stealing, start working, and give. Work creates a bridge between self-centeredness and care for others.

WORK IS MODELED

God Himself stands as our ultimate model. He worked six days and rested on the seventh. Exodus 32:16 talks about the original tablets of the Ten Commandments and says, "The tablets were God's work, and the writing was God's writing."

Deuteronomy 32:4 says, "His work is perfect." In Psalm 111:2-3 we read, "Great are the works of the LORD; they are studied by all who delight in them. Splendid and majestic is His work." Verses 6-8 say, in part, "He has made known to His people the power of His works…The works of His hands are truth and justice…They are upheld forever and ever; they are performed in truth and uprightness."

We, too, represent God's work. He made us. And for those who are in Christ, He has a special ongoing work. In Philippians 1:6, Paul says, "I am confident of this very thing, that He who began a good work in you will perfect it until the day of Christ Jesus."

Earlier we looked at Ephesians 2:10: "We are His workmanship, created in Christ Jesus for good works." We are the work of His hands, and we were created anew in Christ Jesus for the purpose of good works.

God also models work for us. And the Bible points to another entity who models work for us—Proverbs 6:6 says, "Go to the ant, O sluggard"!

Don't you just love the word "sluggard"? I also like how the Holman Christian Standard Bible translates it: "Go to the ant, you slacker!" The New Living Translation says, "Take a lesson from the ants, you lazybones."

The ant, of course, is the opposite of a sluggard. Proverbs 6:6-8 continues, "Observe her ways and be wise, which, having no chief, officer or ruler, prepares her food in the summer and gathers her provision in the harvest."

Human beings are intrinsically lazy. We must be taught otherwise. This passage says to let the ant teach us. "Observe her ways and be wise." The ant has no supervisor. She doesn't need to hear the crack of a whip. If you are a boss, you understand the amazing value of the worker who does not need constant prodding. Godly employees and leaders take the initiative. God values diligence and so will those you work for. Be a good worker; be what you look for in others.

Ants travel in a line. They climb up the side of your house, into a hole you never noticed, then look around the house to see what scraps you left for them. They crawl into your trash can, get a little piece of food, then make the entire journey in reverse all the way back to the nest. No one yells, "Keep it moving, guys! Let's get this done!" The ant "prepares her food in the summer and gathers her provision in the harvest."

During the winter, some ant species eat the food they stored up during the summer, while others merely sleep. But even those that sleep throughout the winter spent their summer eating as much as possible to survive the winter. You probably never thought of an ant putting on weight, but that's what happens. That's one reason why, unlike most insects, cold weather does not kill ants. Ants typically live from 2 to 15 years. Queens live 10 to 30 years.

Work is seasonal. We do different jobs at different times. The blessed man in Psalm 1:3 is "like a tree firmly planted by streams of water, which yields its fruit in its season." Different seasons in your life will result in different work and different kinds of harvest. The key is to stay firmly planted by the streams of what Jesus called "living water" (John 4:10-14; 7:38).

In warm weather, the ant works. During the winter, ants close off the entrances to their nests and most go into hibernation. The ant that was so busy and strong in summer becomes sluggish and slow in the winter.

Seasons change, but they are connected. Your harvest in one season becomes your provision in the next. Don't waste summer and don't waste daylight. In John 9:4, Jesus said, "We must work the works of Him who sent Me as long as it is day; night is coming when no one can work."

That's a spiritual truth, but also a physical one. Don't spend the days and hours of your life on video games or other kinds of activities that yield no harvest. Set aside money. Invest wisely. Think ahead. "Go to the ant, O sluggard, observe her ways and be wise."

WORK IS A PLACE OF GRACE

One way or another, we all serve other people, and people can be unjust. Some are almost always unjust. When you have an unjust boss, work can still be an act of worship. That is because work is also an act of grace.

First Peter 2:18 says, "Servants, be submissive to your masters with all respect, not only to those who are good and gentle, but also to those who are unreasonable." Is your boss unreasonable? Is he or she unfair? Does she take credit for your ideas or your hard work? Does he take advantage of you? As an outworking of God's grace in you, keep on respecting his or her authority. The next verse explains: "This finds favor, if for the sake of conscience toward God a person bears up under sorrows when suffering unjustly" (verse 19).

Consistently doing excellent work, even when you have an unjust boss, reflects God's grace in your life. Imagine yourself alone. You have a job to do. Your boss has been completely unfair to you, and perhaps mean. The work has fallen to you because your boss has been derelict in his or her duty. If you do a bad job, it will not reflect on you but on the boss who has already taken credit. You could ruin him, and pay him back for his arrogance and harm. But instead, you do something superb.

Neither the higher-ups nor your coworkers see it. But Someone sees, and smiles. Don't worry about vengeance or justice. Psalm 37:1 says, "Do not fret because of evildoers." Leave the matter to God. Psalm 37:6 promises, "He will bring forth your righteousness as the light and your judgment as the noonday."

For more help in this area, read Psalms 37 and 73.

WORK IS BLESSED BY GOD

Like his grandfather, Abraham, and his father, Isaac, Jacob was a patriarch of Israel. But he was not always the best person. He tricked his father and cheated his twin brother, Esau. As you can imagine, tension persisted in his family, especially when Esau decided to kill Jacob.

At his mother's suggestion, Jacob went on a journey of about 700 miles to the home of his Uncle Laban. On that journey, he encountered God in a powerful way, and the experience changed his life. When he arrived at Uncle Laban's, he met and quickly fell in love with one of Laban's daughters, Rachel.

After Jacob had been with Laban for a month, the older man said to his nephew, "Because you are my relative, should you therefore serve me for nothing? Tell me, what shall your wages be?" (Genesis 29:15). This tells us that during the first month, even without pay, Jacob had shown himself to be a diligent worker. Laban seemed anxious to tie Jacob's productivity to himself. We see Jacob's response in verse 18: "Now Jacob loved Rachel, so he said, 'I will serve you seven years for your younger daughter Rachel.'"

In other words, Jacob was willing to work and use the payment toward a dowry. You probably know the story. At the end of seven years, Laban tricked Jacob into marrying his older daughter, Leah. He made Jacob work another seven years for Rachel. Ultimately, Jacob ended up serving his uncle for 20 years. In Genesis 31:41, Jacob said to Laban, "These twenty years I have been in your house; I served you fourteen years for your two daughters and six years for your flock, and you changed my wages ten times."

God prospered Jacob through all the adversity. That's why Laban kept breaking his word by lowering Jacob's wages. He thought his nephew was making too much. But God kept pouring out His favor on Jacob.

At the end of the 20 years, Jacob returned to the Promised Land with his wives and children, goats, and sheep. He left home as a poor man but returned with great wealth. In a prayer of thanksgiving, Jacob said to the Lord, "I am unworthy of all the lovingkindness and of all the faithfulness which You have shown to Your servant; for with my staff only I crossed this Jordan" (Genesis 32:10).

Jacob did not inherit material wealth from his prosperous father or grandfather, but from God's blessing on the work of his hands.

THE ULTIMATE WORK

In each of these lessons, we have seen the powerful relationship between work and God. At one point, Jesus revealed the ultimate work:

> Do not work for the food which perishes, but for the food which endures to eternal life, which the Son of Man will give to you, for on Him the Father, God, has set His seal. Therefore they said to Him, "What shall we do, so that we may work the works of God?" Jesus answered and said to

them, "This is the work of God, that you believe in Him whom He has sent" (John 6:27-29).

Jesus' work on the cross allows for all of God's blessings to flow toward us. Have you trusted in Jesus and His work to save you? God calls us to be real men—men who work with diligence.

STUDY QUESTIONS

1. God's normal provision for you will be through work. So why is work so hard and frustrating? Why do managers have a hard time finding great employees? Why do employees have a hard time finding great companies to work for?

2. Does the quality of your work and the level of your effort really matter to God? Read Colossians 3:22–4:1.

3. What can we learn from the ant?

4. Does your employer see Jesus in you and your work? How about your team or your direct reports?

5. If you are a manager and leader, in what ways can you set a healthy, godly work ethic for your staff?

6. Is your work pleasing to God? Is it of such a nature that God can bless it?

PART 8:

REAL MEN RESPECT AUTHORITY

Everyone struggles with submitting to authority. Humans are innately rebellious. Many of us recoil at the thought of humbling ourselves before authority figures. Our pride rejects the idea of yielding to any authority other than our own. Yet we long for the honor and peace God promises to those who correctly submit to authority.

Children, obey your parents in the Lord, for this is right. Honor your father and mother (which is the first commandment with a promise), so that it may be well with you, and that you may live long on the earth.

EPHESIANS 6:1-3

Obey your leaders and submit to them, for they keep watch over your souls as those who will give an account. Let them do this with joy and not with grief, for this would be unprofitable for you.

HEBREWS 13:17

Every person is to be in subjection to the governing authorities. For there is no authority except from God, and those which exist are established by God.

ROMANS 13:1

To disregard parental authority, ecclesiastical authority,
or civil authority is to disregard God's authority.
MARK HENRY

Obedience to lawful authority is
a foundation to manly character.[1]
ROBERT E. LEE

19

UNDERSTANDING AUTHORITY

S cripture has much to say about authority. A good place to start is Matthew 8:5-10:

> When Jesus entered Capernaum, a centurion came to Him, imploring Him, and saying, "Lord, my servant is lying paralyzed at home, fearfully tormented." Jesus said to him, "I will come and heal him." But the centurion said, "Lord, I am not worthy for You to come under my roof, but just say the word, and my servant will be healed. For I also am a man under authority, with soldiers under me; and I say to this one, 'Go!' and he goes, and to another, 'Come!' and he comes, and to my slave, 'Do this!' and he does it." Now when Jesus heard this, He marveled and said to those who were following, "Truly I say to you, I have not found such great faith with anyone in Israel."

From our perspective in the twenty-first century, we read casually about Jesus entering Capernaum and meeting a centurion. But it wasn't casual to people of that time and place. This soldier was a walking, talking symbol of Israel's unwelcome, dictatorial, treacherous, and ruthless occupiers. The Jews surrounding Jesus rightly saw the centurion as dangerous. He needed no probable cause to order a soldier to search a Jew. He could accuse a Jew of a crime for any reason or no reason at all—and that would be that. Even if he happened to be a good guy on a personal level, he was still a hated occupier, and a high-ranking one at that.

Imagine if China attacked the US and put an occupying force here. Then imagine a leader of that occupying force coming to you, asking for a favor. What would you say? It might be "Yes, sir. I'll do anything. Just don't harm my family." Or it might be "Get lost, you evil, red commie!"

THE CENTURION

Jesus was neither intimidated by nor angry with the centurion's request. He treated the Roman like He treated anyone else who came to Him in time of need. He said, "I will come and heal him." The centurion astounded everyone with his response: "Lord, I am not worthy for You to come under my roof."

The centurion commanded some of the best troops in the world at that time. The might of the Roman Empire backed him up. Yet he humbled himself before this itinerant Jewish preacher. He said, "I am not worthy...but just say the word, and my servant will be healed."

Then he expressed his very Roman attitude toward authority. It was an attitude that helped Rome conquer the world. He said, "For I also am a man under authority." He knew authority as a man subject to authority.

He also understood authority as one who wielded it. He said, "I also am a man under authority, with soldiers under me; and I say to this one, 'Go!' and he goes, and to another, 'Come!' and he comes, and to my slave, 'Do this!' and he does it."

He recognized authority in Jesus. That's why he said, "Just say the word, and my servant will be healed." He believed the Lord's authority extended beyond His immediate, physical presence. When Jesus heard these words, He "marveled." He said, "Truly I say to you, I have not found such great faith with anyone in Israel."

AUTHORITY AND WINNING

Understanding authority makes life easier. I'm not talking about being a wimp or knuckling under to bullies. I'm talking about a biblical perspective on leadership and being a follower. An NFL player may make more money than his position coach, or even his head coach. But great players listen and learn. Great teams are full of players who buy into their coaches' teachings.

A given player might have tens of thousands of social media followers. He might have millions of children who look up to him and want to emulate him. But he is also a man under authority. No matter how skilled the player, no matter how famous, how rich, or how loved, he must submit to the authority of the coaches, the game officials, and the league. A player's ability to navigate both leadership and submission allows him to go from being a guy with great talent to being a genuinely great player. And it allows teams to go from losing to winning.

Understanding authority helps you understand when to lead and when to follow. It helps you know when to express a dissenting opinion. It also helps you work with all your might to make the team successful—even when you think the leader is making a strategic error. Know when to put in your two cents and when to march toward enemy fire even when you think you know a better way.

HUPOTASSO—IN SUBJECTION

Again, the Bible has much to say about authority. It begins with God's authority over all things. It goes on to speak of human authority, including parental authority, workplace authority, church authority, and civil authority. Romans 13:1 tells us "to be in subjection to the governing authorities." "In subjection" is a translation of the Greek word *hupotasso*, which means "to rank under someone" or "to follow someone." Even though Jesus was the Lord of the universe and His parents didn't fully understand Him, Luke 2:51 says that Jesus remained "in subjection"—*hupotasso*—to them.

Romans 10:3 speaks of people trying to establish their own righteousness and refusing to subject (*hupotasso*) themselves to the righteousness of God. First Corinthians 16:16 uses the same word to talk about subjecting ourselves to church leaders. That doesn't mean blind obedience to everything you hear from the pulpit. It means having respect for the leader's ecclesiastical position and authority in Christ.

Finally, Ephesians 1:22 addresses the authority of Christ: "He put all things in subjection [*hupotasso*] under His feet."

LAW-ABIDING REVOLUTIONARIES

While you should not be looking for an out, you need to understand that a person or a government with authority over you might order you to sin. The boss might ask you to cheat a customer. The government might prohibit you from spreading the gospel. In such situations, having godly character will help you to make the right decision in advance. You will not cheat the customer. You will not lie. You will not keep silent about the good news of Jesus Christ. The statutes of God trump the orders of men.

Corrie ten Boom's father, Casper, saw Nazis taking Jews to death camps in railroad cars. He hid a group of them, putting himself and his family in mortal danger. Later, Corrie would tell their story in her classic book *The Hiding Place*. These things still happen, and they will continue to do so until Jesus returns. You could be faced with a decision as momentous as Casper ten Boom's. So decide now: I follow Jesus, the Son of God!

Acts 5:29 says that when Jewish authorities ordered the apostles to stop preaching and teaching about Jesus, they answered, "We must obey God rather than men." This was not high-handed defiance. They were not disrespectful. Verse 26 says the authorities brought them in "without violence." They were able to bring them in without violence because the apostles did not resist. They showed respect. They did not start a riot or encourage the crowd to burn down the neighborhood. Their defiance was limited to the area of conflict between the Sanhedrin's orders and God's.

The disciples understood authority and, even when they had to disobey it, they still respected it. At this point, the story gets rough. Peter and the others were badly beaten! The authorities flogged them and again ordered them not to speak in the name of Jesus. Finally, they released the disciples.

Then a miracle happened. Acts 5:41-42 says, "So they went on their way from the presence of the Council, rejoicing that they had been considered worthy to suffer shame for His name. And every day, in the temple and from house to house, they kept right on teaching and preaching Jesus as the Christ."

That's not normal, but it is *Christian*. With their backs still bleeding and their whole bodies sick from shock, they went on their way rejoicing. "Hallelujah! We have been considered worthy to suffer shame for His name!"

None of us want to be beaten up. None of them did either. We don't want to live through those kinds of punishment or in those kinds of times. But we do live in such times. As of January 2021, Open

Doors, a relief organization serving persecuted Christians, estimated that 340 million Christians faced persecution for their faith.[1] That's one in eight believers worldwide!

You will face severe tests of faith. That is why it is so important to put the Man Code into practice now. Satan teaches men to glorify lawlessness. Across the world today, he has engineered societies where *subversive* has become a synonym for *heroic*.

Followers of Christ are not lawless. Early Christians "turned the world upside down" (Acts 17:6 NKJV). But they staged their revolution as law-abiding citizens of heaven.

IN GRACE

Submitting to human laws and human authority does not limit your opportunities. The Roman centurion was not born a centurion; he grew into that position. He served faithfully for eight to ten years before receiving that rank. Godly submission does not mean the subordinate must remain in that same role for life. Rather, it provides the path to opportunity. It is the route to move up into greater esteem, honor, leadership, responsibilities, and duties.

We are all under someone's authority. The questions are these: Are we defiant, like Satan, or do we honor God in submission? Is it a faith issue, and can I trust God to bless me in submission? Even though we will always be accountable to someone, we can expect godly character, focused ambition, a willingness to assume responsibility, and the other essentials of the Man Code to bring an increase in our own authority.

SUBJECT TO MEN, PROTECTED BY GOD

I remember the first time I really thought about Romans 13:1, which says, "Every person is to be in subjection to the governing authorities." I automatically added a caveat: "I'll be subject to governing authorities as long as they are good."

There is a major flaw in that kind of thinking. If you subject yourself only to "good" governing authorities, you will never subject yourself to a human government. I believe the United States of America has long been a light among nations and a blessing to the world. Yet it is also full of sin and moral failings, and we're seeing it in spiritual and moral decline. But regardless of what you think about the government, as a citizen of the United States, the Bible says you are subject to the United States and its representatives.

As a Christian, you carry dual citizenship. Philippians 3:20 says, "Our citizenship is in heaven." When Paul wrote those words, he was a citizen of Israel, Rome, and heaven. He took seriously the rights and responsibilities of all three. He subjected himself to all three governing authorities. The highest of the three was his citizenship in heaven. That took priority over Israel and Rome, but it did not negate his submission to Israel and Rome.

SUBJECTS OF NERO

Paul wrote Romans 13 when Nero ruled the Roman Empire.

An article in ListVerse by Patrick Ryan summarizes Nero quite well: "He poisoned, beheaded, stabbed, burned, boiled, crucified and impaled people. He often raped women and cut off the veins and private parts of both men and women…Thousands of Christians were starved to death, burned, torn by dogs, fed to lions, crucified, used as torches, and nailed to crosses."[1]

When Paul wrote Romans 13:1, Nero reigned as the ultimate human governing authority on earth. That closes the door on the excuse, "But it's an evil government, so I don't have to submit."

In Mark 12:13-17, the Pharisees tried to trap Jesus with a question about human authority. They asked Him if they should pay taxes to Caesar. Jesus answered, "'Bring Me a denarius to look at.' They brought one. And He said to them, 'Whose likeness and inscription is this?' And they said to Him, 'Caesar's.' And Jesus said to them, 'Render to Caesar the things that are Caesar's, and to God the things that are God's.'"

For us, the lesson is simple. Pay your taxes. And follow the laws of human government as long as they do not contradict the law of God.

REASONS TO BE SUBJECT
TO THE GOVERNMENT

1. *God tells us to.* We just looked at Romans 13:1. It and other verses command us to be in subjection to governing authorities.

2. *Subjection to government is a form of subjection to God.* The second half of Romans 13:1 says, "There is no authority except from God, and those which exist are established by God."

3. *Governments rise and fall according to the providence of God.* Daniel 2:21 says that God "removes kings and establishes kings." In John 19:11, Jesus stood before Pontius Pilate, the Roman governor of Judea, and said to him, "You would have no authority over Me, unless it had been given you from above."

WHY WOULD GOD APPOINT AN EVIL GOVERNMENT?

God sometimes graciously gives nations the leaders they need. Other times, He justly gives them the leaders they deserve. Isaiah 3:4-5 illustrates this. God sometimes replaces wise and honorable leaders. In their place, He says, "I will make mere lads their princes, and capricious children will rule over them, and the people will be oppressed, each one by another, and each one by his neighbor."

"Capricious children" are impulsive. They give in to rage, and they lack self-control. Evil leaders are a judgment from God. But during such regimes, remember God's promises. They remain true and valid for His people, no matter who leads the government.

Romans 13:4-5 describes God's good purpose for government. Governing authorities are to suppress evil, thus allowing citizens to live in peace. Governments are to protect us—even though imperfectly—from thieves, rapists, murderers, and other evildoers. There may be aspects of a government that you despise. God may also despise those things. But the government is still there to preserve and protect you and those you love.

21

THE SPIRITUAL WORK
OF SUBMISSION

The apostle Peter also wrote about submission to governing authorities:

> Submit [*hupotasso*] yourselves for the Lord's sake to every human institution, whether to a king as the one in authority, or to governors as sent by him for the punishment of evildoers and the praise of those who do right. For such is the will of God that by doing right you may silence the ignorance of foolish men...Honor all people, love the brotherhood, fear God, honor the king (1 Peter 2:13-15, 17).

Who reigned when Peter wrote this passage? Nero—the guy who fed Christians to wild dogs and used them as human torches to light his garden.

This admonition affects actions, but it starts with attitudes. As mentioned earlier, there is an exception to the rule about obeying every governmental command. But even in civil disobedience, we should remain civil. The Greek word translated "honor" in verse 17 above carries a connotation of valuing, even prizing. We should prize people, even the king.

If that sounds impossible, remember that the Holy Spirit who inspired these verses of Scripture also works in us and through us. When you and I honor someone's authority, even if that person is not honorable, it becomes a spiritual work of grace—*His work!*

PRAY AND EXPECT CHANGE

First Timothy 2:1-2 says, "I urge that entreaties and prayers, petitions and thanksgivings, be made on behalf of all men, for kings and all who are in authority, so that we may lead a tranquil and quiet life in all godliness and dignity."

You've heard the expression "Prayer changes things." It *does* change things, starting with us. When you and I start praying for those in authority—even those who persecute the people we love—it shifts our perspective, quiets the soul, and prepares us to live godly lives whatever may befall us. Our anger melts into compassion and godly pity. It is here, in this space, that God's grace flows into the hearts of His servants.

We must still speak the truth. For instance, we must still condemn a nation's sin. We must say with boldness, "God will hold this nation accountable for its sin!" But we must also speak with kindness and care, illustrating the love of Christ, who longs not to judge but to save.

PRAY AND EXPECT MORE CHANGE

Not only does praying for wicked authority figures change us, it also has the potential to change them. You want yourself, your family, and your friends to live life in peace, prosperity, and security, even if the political party you oppose comes into power. That's a fantastic reason to pray for your national and community leaders, despite party affiliation. Pray for their enlightenment and understanding. Pray for them to have wisdom and that they will oppose corruption. Pray that they use their power as God intends. Upheavals caused by ungodly leadership make it difficult to lead quiet and tranquil lives. So pray that leaders will come to faith in Christ and increase in godliness.

Psalm 63:3 says that God's "lovingkindness is better than life." Praying for those in authority helps us step into a realm of living where God's lovingkindness is manifest in everything we do and every bit of who we are.

THE MAN WHO SUBMITTED AND RULED

Daniel was an alien in a foreign land...just like we are.

According to Philippians 3:20, if you know Jesus, your "citizenship is in heaven." You are an alien passing through a land that probably seems stranger to you by the day. Admittedly, we can start to feel at home here. But there is always a sense of being out of place. And as the world's rebellion against God increases, so does the Christian's sense of displacement.

Daniel spent his entire life as a foreigner. The Babylonians captured him and took him from his homeland when he was a young teen. The first chapter of the book of Daniel tells the story. The conquerors identified Daniel as gifted. They placed him in a special program that turned talented foreigners into loyal, useful Babylonians.

When the Babylonians took a people captive, they looked for intelligent, educated, talented, and handsome young men who showed promise of becoming leaders. Under King Nebuchadnezzar, they saw talent as a major part of the treasure they plundered from conquered peoples. They immersed these young men in the language and culture of Babylon. They removed them from their families, dressed them like Babylonians, gave them new names, flattered them, and threatened them. It was a powerful and lengthy course in what we now call brainwashing.

GODLY LIVING IN AN EVIL GENERATION

Through all of this, Daniel and his friends remembered God and His laws. In part 4 of this book, we looked at the story of Daniel's friends—Shadrach, Meshach, and Abed-nego. We saw their devotion to God even when faced with death in a fiery furnace.

Like the captives from other lands, these four young Hebrews were supposed to eat the food and drink the wine prepared in the king's own kitchens. That would have been the highest quality cuisine available. Receiving it was considered an honor. But that food was not kosher.

Daniel and his friends wanted to keep a clear conscience before God. Daniel 1:8 says, "Daniel made up his mind that he would not defile himself with the king's choice food or with the wine which he drank; so he sought permission from the commander of the officials that he might not defile himself."

Daniel did not go into a rage and make a big show of his virtue. He didn't shout, "I will not defile myself with your king's filthy food!" He "sought permission...of the officials." He respected their authority. He asked if he and his friends could eat vegetables only. God's law did not require Daniel to be vegetarian, but he knew the meat would not be prepared in the manner God had laid out in the law of Moses. Vegetables were the safe way to go.

King Nebuchadnezzar had a reputation for removing the heads of the people who defied him. The official in charge of the young men feared that if they only ate vegetables, Daniel and his friends would appear sickly. If the king saw them looking worse than the boys from other captive lands, it might cost this man more than his job. It could cost his life.

Daniel did not argue or harangue. This teen Hebrew laid out a reasonable proposal, one that the official could try without endangering himself before the king. Daniel said, "Please test your servants for ten days, and let us be given some vegetables to eat and water to drink. Then let our appearance be observed in your presence and the appearance of the youths who are eating the king's choice food; and deal with your servants according to what you see" (Daniel 1:12-13).

The official agreed to this. At the end of the ten days, Daniel and his friends looked better and healthier than the young men eating food from the king's kitchen.

BEHEADING WISE GUYS

Two years later, King Nebuchadnezzar began to have a recurring dream, and it troubled him. The king took his problem to his wise men and sages. He told them to tell him the dream and its interpretation. The king seemed to sense the dream's significance, and he wanted to understand its meaning. So to make sure that the wise men knew what they were talking about, he demanded that they not only interpret the dream, but also describe it.

According to Daniel 2:3-4, "The king said to them, 'I had a dream and my spirit is anxious to understand the dream.' Then the Chaldeans spoke to the king in Aramaic: 'O king, live forever! Tell the dream to your servants, and we will declare the interpretation.'"

The king did not like this answer. He said, "The command from me is firm: if you do not make known to me the dream and its interpretation, you will be torn limb from limb and your houses will be made a rubbish heap" (verse 5).

In response, the wise men told him, in effect, "That's not fair. Kings are supposed to tell wise men their dreams, and then wise men tell the king what the dreams mean." The king replied, in effect, "We're about to make some cutbacks around here, starting with your necks!"

DISCRETION AND DISCERNMENT

At this time, Daniel was still quite young, but his talent and training made him one of the wise men. He worked in that department of government, so the king's order to execute the wise men would have included him.

Daniel 2:13-15 says what happened next:

> The decree went forth that the wise men should be slain; and they looked for Daniel and his friends to kill them. Then Daniel replied with discretion and discernment to Arioch, the captain of the king's bodyguard, who had gone forth to slay the wise men of Babylon; he said to Arioch, the king's commander, "For what reason is the decree from the king so urgent?" Then Arioch informed Daniel about the matter.

You would expect Daniel to panic, run, and hide. Instead, he sought out the man sent to execute him and reasoned with him. He spoke "with discretion and discernment." He understood Arioch's position. Daniel did not rail about the foolishness of killing all the king's counselors. He seized on the point that must also have disturbed Arioch. Why so urgent? The order didn't seem thought out or strategic. A military man like Arioch would have wanted everything done with care and deliberation. Killing all the king's counselors so suddenly would be a purge from which Nebuchadnezzar, and perhaps Babylon itself, could not recover.

Daniel's "discretion and discernment," along with his poise and courage, paid off. Arioch gave him time to seek an answer. "Then Daniel went to his house and informed his friends, Hananiah, Mishael and Azariah, about the matter" (verse 17).

The four teenagers went to God in prayer. A looming death penalty can give prayer a special urgency. So, I'm sure it was what the book of James 5:16 calls "fervent prayer" (KJV).

THE YOUNG MAN SPEAKS TO THE KING

We then read that "the mystery was revealed to Daniel in a night vision" (Daniel 2:19). After that, you might expect the young man to send out a press release that he knew both the dream and the interpretation. Shout it in the streets. Go to the palace, crow a bit. But even as a teen, Daniel really was a wise man. He and his friends prayed again, this time in thanksgiving and praise.

Later that morning, young Daniel stood before Nebuchadnezzar—a teenage foreigner before the most powerful man in the world. He did not toot his own horn. He began by testifying of the one true God. Daniel said, "As for the mystery about which the king has inquired, neither wise men, conjurers, magicians nor diviners are able to declare it to the king. However, there is a God in heaven who reveals mysteries, and He has made known to King Nebuchadnezzar what will take place in the latter days" (verses 27-28).

Daniel told the king the dream and the interpretation. Before doing so, Daniel honored God. The king's response also gave honor to God, as well as to young Daniel.

> King Nebuchadnezzar fell on his face and did homage
> to Daniel, and gave orders to present to him an offering
> and fragrant incense. The king answered Daniel and said,

"Surely your God is a God of gods and a Lord of kings and a revealer of mysteries, since you have been able to reveal this mystery." Then the king promoted Daniel and gave him many great gifts, and he made him ruler over the whole province of Babylon and chief prefect over all the wise men of Babylon. And Daniel made request of the king, and he appointed Shadrach, Meshach and Abednego over the administration of the province of Babylon, while Daniel was at the king's court (verses 46-49).

Daniel understood the concept of prayer, honor, and submission. Even in a terrifying situation, he remained faithful, and God honored him.

CHOOSING FAITH OVER BITTERNESS

The dream's interpretation turned out to be personally flattering to King Nebuchadnezzar. That probably made the harsher parts of the prophecy go down easier. Later in life, Daniel would find himself in the opposite situation. He would tell King Belshazzar that he had been weighed in the balance and found wanting; that his kingdom was about to be overthrown, and that it was all because of his own sin. Despite the harsh nature of God's message to Belshazzar, Daniel apparently spoke with respect because when he finished, Belshazzar, too, honored Daniel by putting him in royal garments and giving him a fantastic promotion (Daniel 5:29).

The promotion would last only a few hours. Shortly after it was given, the army of Darius the Mede[1] captured Babylon and executed King Belshazzar. With this change of rulers, Daniel again faced a new culture, a new regime, and a new king.

Daniel honored this new king. But when a royal decree conflicted with God's orders, Daniel risked his life by obeying God instead of man. He maintained his respectfulness toward the king even as the king's men threw him in a den of lions. Then, to the king's delight, God kept Daniel safe.

Everyone struggles with submission to authority. Daniel's life had been upended by a people full of evil. There may have been times when he wanted to torch the famous hanging gardens of Babylon. Psalm 137 describes the feelings of Israeli captives on their forced journey from Jerusalem to Babylon. Verse 9 gives us a vivid picture of the captives' rage and grief: "How blessed will be the one who seizes and dashes your little ones against the rock."

That's a picture of the anger and anguish the Israelis felt as the Babylonians prodded them and mocked them on their way to a foreign land. But instead of acting out in bitterness and frustration, Daniel chose faith in God. He became an archetype who showed Jews the means to flourishing during the diaspora (the displacement of Jews from Israel) around the world for thousands of years.

We are all innately rebellious. We recoil at the thought of humbling ourselves before authority figures—especially if they are in some way alien to us. But God has a better way. He promises peace and strength to those who correctly submit to authority.

Remember 1 Corinthians 16:13: Act like men! Real men respect authority.

STUDY QUESTIONS

1. Who created authority and the order of governance? Who holds all authorities accountable? How should leaders respond to this?

2. Which of the passages on honoring authority gripped you the most? Why? Which Bible story helps you the most—the centurion, Daniel, or...?

3. In your current phase of life, what authorities has God put over you? What is your spirit toward them? Are you honoring them in ways that please God?

4. What are you teaching your children and others about authority? Are you directly or indirectly teaching them to be rebels? How will this affect you (and them) in the future?

5. Satan is lawless and a rebel. Ask yourself: *Have I positioned myself to experience God's blessing in my life with regard to my following and leading? What do I need to change to be successful in God's eyes?*

PART 9:

REAL MEN HONOR THEIR WIVES

Real men honor their wives. We live in a culture that cringes at the idea of biological differences between men and women, or gender-specific roles of any kind. Nature and Scripture tell us otherwise. God calls men to deal with their wives gently, considerately, and with honor. (Not married? Check the end of this section to see how this part of the Man Code applies to you.)

In Scripture, we are given these reminders:

> *He who finds a wife finds a good thing and*
> *obtains favor from the Lord.*
> PROVERBS 18:22

> *Let your fountain be blessed, and rejoice in the wife of your*
> *youth. As a loving hind and a graceful doe, let her breasts*
> *satisfy you at all times; be exhilarated always with her love.*
> PROVERBS 5:18-19

A happy marriage is the union of two good forgivers.[1]
ROBERT QUILLEN

*Great marriages don't happen by luck or by accident. They are
the result of a consistent investment of time, thoughtfulness,
forgiveness, affection, prayer, mutual respect, and a rock-
solid commitment between a husband and a wife.*[2]
DAVE WILLIS

23

HONOR YOUR WIFE

If you want to be able to walk into any situation with godly confidence and authority, start that journey by honoring your wife. Earlier, we looked at Jesus washing His disciple's feet. He said it was an example for us. How much more should we wash the feet of our wives spiritually! Do that, and when you stand up, you will stand taller in Christ.

There's a powerful word for us in 1 Peter 3:7: "You husbands in the same way, live with your wives in an understanding way, as with someone weaker, since she is a woman; and show her honor as a fellow heir of the grace of life, so that your prayers will not be hindered."

Honor your wife. She is a fellow heir "of the grace of life." She is Jesus' lovely daughter. He laid down His life for her. You can either build her up or tear her down. If you tear her down, you answer to God.

Do you want your prayers unhindered? Honor your wife! Men can honor their wives in many ways. Here are a few.

HONOR YOUR WIFE IN PRAYER

Praying for one another is not only an expression of love, but an amplifier of love. When we pray for or with others, we enter their

struggles, difficulties, emotional lows and emotional highs, temptations, and triumphs. Saying, "Let me pray for you" is not a put-down
or a put-on. It is a builder-upper!

Do not just pray for your wife. Pray *with* her. It's likely that no one
will agree with you in prayer more perfectly (Matthew 18:19). And
nothing will bring a deeper level of intimacy and love than pouring out
your hearts together in worship, supplication, and submission to God.

HONOR YOUR WIFE WITH WORDS

It is crucial that we honor our wives with the words we use when we
speak to and about them. The old comedic standby "Take my wife…
please" isn't all that funny when you think about it. Some men use
jokes as if they were billy clubs. I'm not saying you can't tell jokes,
but when you do, be ever cognizant that even in kidding around, it's
your job to honor your wife.

First Thessalonians 5:11 tells Christians to "build up one another."
If that applies to all your brothers and sisters in Christ, how much
more does it apply to your wife? Build her up. Don't tear her down.
And remember that nothing builds up or tears down quite like the
tongue (James 3:1-10).

Think of the words you use when you talk about your wife to
your children or to the people at work or to your parents or siblings.
Do your words honor the woman God has made your lifelong part-
ner? Say things that honor her. Say them about her and to her. You
are accountable to God for how you use words regarding your wife.

HONOR YOUR WIFE WITH DEEDS

Jera and I bought our first house in Parachute, Colorado. The house
was built in 1922. It had been used as a mining shack in Aspen. Later,

it was moved 180 miles to Parachute. When we bought the little house, it was the cheapest one on the market.

When you buy the cheapest house, you have to expect problems. Three days after moving in, our daughter hit the metal siding of the house with a steel rake. Sparks flew, and smoke started rising. Jera called me at the church office, "The house is going to burn down!" I did what you would do—I raced home, got Jera and the children to safety, and cut the electrical wires that connected the house to the power pole.

Truly, by the grace of God, no one was hurt. The house, however... well, let's just say it needed a lot of tender-loving care.

My actions in the moment of crisis honored Jera and her needs, but it was the years that followed that were the hardest. We had a long list of repairs to be made: install complete electrical service to the house, rewire the house, re-insulate it, vent the attic, etc. Jera also had a long "honey-do" list: a new bedroom addition, a dishwasher, fresh paint, a second bathroom, etc.

In the long run, watching a football game has little consequence. But doing the "honey-do" list has eternal consequences because in doing those things, we honor our wives. God smiles. And He answers our prayers.

HONOR YOUR WIFE WITH YOUR AFFECTIONS

What do you really love? Football, hunting, basketball, running, fishing, working out, skiing, golfing, barbequing, doing your job? You can tell what you love by what you think about, what you spend time and money on, and what you enjoy talking about the most. The next question is even more important: Do you love your wife more than these things? Does she know it? Does she feel it?

Jesus commands us to love our neighbors. That is clearly defined in the Bible. We do them good, not evil. We don't lie, steal, or harm them. How much more our wives? The New Testament emphasizes that our deepest affection is to be toward her.

It's easy to focus our affections in the wrong places. The Bible is clear. Setting your affection on your wife—always second to God, but still real affection—is not one of the wrong places. Ephesians 5:25 could not be clearer about the affection a man should feel for his wife. It tells us plainly: "Husbands, love your wives."

HONOR YOUR WIFE WITH YOUR EYES

We live in seductive times. Bawdiness, carnality, and various levels of pornography have made their way into almost everything.

The Bible tells us that Job was a righteous man before God. He feared God and walked with Him. And like all men, he was tested by Satan. Job faced several difficult trials, only to be insulted by his friends. In Job's last defense of his own devotion to God, he spoke of a covenant he had made before God; it was a promise to guard his eyes: "I made a covenant with my eyes not to look with lust at a young woman" (Job 31:1 NLT).

In Matthew 5:27-28, Jesus said, "You have heard that it was said, 'You shall not commit adultery'; but I say to you that everyone who looks at a woman with lust for her has already committed adultery with her in his heart."

In every generation, men will be tempted to desire other women. It is a battle they will face. Satan is hunting for you today. He wants you to dishonor God and your wife. In this way, countless marriages and lives have been destroyed. Do not be another casualty in the spiritual war. Make a covenant with your eyes and so honor your wife. Turn your desire toward your wife alone.

HONOR YOUR WIFE IN YOUR PLANS

Jera and I love to go out for pizza. Pizza gloriously enhances a mar-riage—at least, that's how it works for us. While we're out, I ask her what's on her bucket list. "What are your hopes? What's important to you? What do you want to do next, and what after that?"

I want to honor Jera in my plans. To do that, we must plan together, dream together, set goals together. It's not *my* show. It's ours. It's not *my* life. It's ours. We're in this together, so I honor her by planning with her and giving her desires a priority equal to those of my own.

HONOR YOUR WIFE WITH YOUR LIFE

I want to honor God with my life. And I want to honor Jera. My conduct—the things I say and how I carry myself—all reflect on Jera. I will either bring honor to God and honor to Jera, or I will bring shame to God and shame to my wife. Don't do anything that will bring shame to your wife. Let everything about your life bring her honor and respect.

Think about the disgraced politician caught in a sexual entangle-ment with an intern, standing at a podium and confessing to the pub-lic while assuring them that he will be a changed man in the future. It will never happen again. There at his side, in embarrassment, shame, and dishonor, stands his wife. You may not be a politician, but your way of living still reflects on your wife. Make that reflection bright and shining, not dark, tawdry, or debased.

This is not just about big, public things. We also honor our wives in thousands of little ways. Years ago, some nice ladies in the church I pastored at the time came to me with a suggestion. "Pastor Mark, we've been talking, and we think you would be a lot more handsome if you would shave off your beard."

I think they would have been willing to take up an offering to buy me a razor! But they could not persuade me. The decision was not in their hands, or even in mine. I said to them, "Jera likes my face this way. If Jera likes me this way, I will stay this way." Simply put, Jera's preferences are to be honored before anyone else's.

Recently I had lunch with a fellow pastor. He was a well-built and fit man, and I couldn't help but try to fatten him up. I tried to give him some food with carbs. He said, "No, I can't eat any of that."

"Why not?" I asked, thinking perhaps he had food allergies. He said, "I'm trying to make sure I have a great physique for my wife." He honored his wife even in the way he chose to eat. He lived intentionally to honor her.

Real men honor their wives.

24

REFLECTIONS FOR SINGLES

Men, this is the reality: All of us start life being single, and many of us will end this life being single. The man of God who has the gift of singleness can lead a rich and meaningful life even though he never marries or raises children of his own. If this is your calling from God, then do it well! Jesus lived this life of singleness and so did others, like John the Baptist. Follow their example and live in a holy way. Use your singleness as a platform to advance the gospel of Jesus Christ. The Scriptures are clear: Singleness is not a curse, but a level of opportunity that married friends are unable to enjoy. The apostle Paul put it this way:

> I want you to be free from concern. One who is unmarried
> is concerned about the things of the Lord, how he may
> please the Lord; but one who is married is concerned about
> the things of the world, how he may please his wife, and
> his interests are divided. The woman who is unmarried,
> and the virgin, is concerned about the things of the Lord,

that she may be holy both in body and spirit; but one
who is married is concerned about the things of the world,
how she may please her husband (1 Corinthians 7:32-34).

Notice that the single person has a singular concern: how to please the Lord. The married person (sometimes) walks this tension of pleasing the Lord and his or her spouse. This divided interest is a normal part of the marriage relationship and takes a lot of energy and wisdom. If you are single, use this season wisely, and don't be given to the selfish pursuits of those who don't know Christ. Rather, use the gift for God's pursuits.

YOUNG MEN

When I was in ninth grade, I was called into the principal's office. I had no idea what I had done; I was scared out of my mind. Mr. O'Brien invited me to take a seat and started with some small talk. My curiosity was killing me! My mind was racing and wondering, *Henry, what did you do wrong?*

After an eternity of five minutes, Mr. O'Brien started telling me about his teen and college years. He told me of his faith and commitment to Christ. He shared a golden nugget of wisdom with me about his devotion to his future wife. I can still see him sitting at his desk and still hear his words: "I purposed being single to honor God and my future wife by never touching or kissing another woman. She will be the first woman I kiss; the only woman I ever kiss."

Leaning forward in his chair for emphasis, he looked me in the eye and said, "I made it through those years, and the one and only woman I have ever kissed is my wife, Sue. Your actions today will honor God and your future wife, or they will dishonor God and your future wife. Honor God. Honor her."

This kind of advice may sound insane in our lust-driven world, but remember the wisdom of Mr. O'Brien: Your actions today matter.

Honor your future wife today by resolving to be sexually pure with guarded eyes and mind, by mastering the skills in the workplace to be able to financially provide, by managing your finances so as not to burden her future, by developing skills in household management and repair, by acquiring wisdom in decision making and self-denial, by learning the Scriptures and serving in ministry, by gaining the insight of heaven regarding marriage and family life, and by living a life of humility, forgiveness, and service toward others.

If God blesses you with a wife in the future, when do you start to honor her? You start today.

DIVORCED MEN

"This is not what I had envisioned for my marriage," said Joe with tears in his eyes. "Julie's high school boyfriend found her on social media and wants her back. She told me that they had been intimate through their senior year of high school and at different seasons throughout college. She married me only to get back at him for cheating on her in college. Well, he is recently divorced and wants Julie back. I have begged her to consider what this will do to Christ's reputation, what it will do to our children, and what it is doing to me. She is filing for a divorce today."

You might have a story like Joe's. You did not want a divorce. And some of you who are reading these words wanted the divorce and initiated it. There are a lot of variables behind why divorce takes place, but let me share a few general thoughts that may help you.

If your ex-wife has not remarried, and you have not remarried, seek reconciliation with her. This honors God and it honors her. Ask some good men to join you in fasting and prayer for the restoration of your marriage. I have seen this happen!

If your ex-wife has remarried or if you have remarried, first, commit to never speak ill of her before your children and others. Second, as much as it depends on you, deal peaceably with her. Third, never take revenge. And last, honor her with a forgiving spirit. This will honor Christ and put you in the best position for His blessing.

Are you single again? Should you remarry? Maybe. I would encourage you to get wise counsel from a godly pastor. Every situation is complex; life is complicated. As I reflect on Matthew 19 and 1 Corinthians 7, it seems clear to me that remarriage is a possibility for situations where immorality or abandonment were the cause of the divorce. If you are divorced and single again, get wise counsel, take time to heal, and use this time wisely to prepare for the future. Take a few minutes and read or reread the previous section written to young men. You'll know the content that applies to you.

WIDOWERS

Proverbs 31:10 says, "An excellent wife, who can find? For her worth is far above jewels."

Ron sat weeping across from me. His wife had gone to be with Christ four months earlier. They had been married almost 45 years. His words still touch me: "I am so alone. She was a gift from God." This was the very reason God created marriage in Genesis 2; it was not good for Adam to be alone.

How do you honor your wife now? First, Proverbs 31 talks about how a godly woman is to be praised by her husband and her children. I would encourage you to write down her virtues and her greatest acts of faith, devotion, love, and service to her God. Let these be the stories you share about her to your children, grandchildren, and friends.

Second, remember that life is not over for you. In 2019, Dr. Tony Evans lost his dear wife, Lois, to cancer. In an article in *Decision* magazine, Dr. Evans described the gift God had given him in Lois and her spiritual legacy, which reaches around the world. He also elaborated on his journey of grief. It is a powerful article, but my personal takeaway was when Dr. Evans wrote, "My teammate is gone...But I'm gonna keep blocking and tackling. I'll miss my teammate, but the game of God's kingdom must go on."[1]

If your beloved wife has preceded you to heaven, friend, the game is still on for you! Honor her with stories of her acts of faith and honor her by staying in the game. Get up and get on the field, and run the next play!

STUDY QUESTIONS

1. Do you see your wife as a gift from God? Why or why not?

2. There are many ways you can honor your wife. List three ways that would mean the most to her right now (you might need to ask her over dinner).

3. How should the fear of God affect your marriage relationship? What are the immediate benefits and eternal benefits of honoring your wife?

4. Any fool can have a dysfunctional marriage. Any fool can have an affair. Any fool can leave his wife. Real men honor their wives and build strong marriages. What kind of man will you be? What are your next three steps to honoring your wife?

5. If you are currently single:

   a. How do you, as a single man, honor your future wife? What are the three easiest ways to honor her today? What are the three hardest? Why does this matter?

b. How is it possible for a widower to honor his wife? Give some examples.

c. Why should a single man be thinking about how to honor his future wife? Is this part of "real men pursing biblical success"? Why or why not?

PART 10

REAL MEN TRAIN THEIR CHILDREN

Real men take responsibility for the upbringing and training of their little ones. They know they must fulfill God's calling on them as fathers. This includes not provoking or agitating their children to anger, but instead, disciplining and instructing them in the Lord (Ephesians 6:4). (No kids? Check the end of this section to see how this part of the Man Code applies to you.)

Here are two other passages that reveal the great importance of good parenting:

You, however, continue in the things you have learned and become convinced of, knowing from whom you have learned them, and that from childhood you have known the sacred writings which are able to give you the wisdom that leads to salvation through faith which is in Christ Jesus.

2 TIMOTHY 3:14-15

Correct your son, and he will give you comfort; he will also delight your soul.

PROVERBS 29:17

We cannot always build the future for our youth,
but we can build our youth for the future.[1]
FRANKLIN D. ROOSEVELT

Godly parents have often been afflicted with wicked children;
grace does not run in the blood, but corruption does.[2]
MATTHEW HENRY

25

DISCIPLINE AND INSTRUCTION

Most people think of influencers as beautiful young people who have become lifestyle gurus to their hundreds of thousands (or even millions) of social media followers. But we are all influencers. And every day presents new opportunities to influence others—especially children—for God.

Jera and I are empty nesters. But the job of influencing children does not end when the last of your brood heads out on his or her own. Though our kids no longer depend on us, we still influence our thirtysomething-year-old children as they raise their own kids. We influence grandsons. We influence children in our church, and even the kids we see when we stand in line at Walmart.

A dad's most profound influence happens in the home. Real men train their children.

A FATHER'S UNIQUE ROLE IN TEACHING

Ephesians 5:25 says, "Husbands, love your wives." A few verses later, in Ephesians 6:4, men get another fundamental lesson in family.

This one speaks to the man's role in parenting: "Fathers, do not provoke your children to anger, but bring them up in the discipline and instruction of the Lord."

When a father provokes a child to anger, he creates in that child a deep and abiding frustration. Such frustrations can sometimes last throughout life. Don't prod your children to anger, either in the name of fun or as discipline. The rest of the verse makes clear that men must discipline their kids, but not by toying with their emotional well-being. Never intentionally agitate, provoke, or enrage your kids. Don't be a bully. Don't humiliate or demean. When dads do that, the pain can be life-damaging.

After telling fathers what not to do, Ephesians 6:4 tells them what to do: "Bring [your children] up in the discipline and instruction of the Lord." It does not say to bring them up in "the discipline and instruction" of hockey, football, movie watching, video gaming, tomahawk throwing, or fly-fishing. "Bring them up in the discipline and instruction of the Lord"!

Whatever your economic background or culture, this is a priority of real men. You might think your wife is better at disciplining and instructing the children. If it seems that way, then you married well. But that does not remove the unique responsibility God has given to you as a father.

Some husband-and-wife tasks can be delegated to the one who is better at it. Not this one. Both parents handle this, especially the father. You must assume responsibility here! Direct, teach, and encourage your children in ways that will help them become followers of Jesus.

Discipline

The original New Testament Greek word translated "discipline" conveys the idea of giving instruction and meting out appropriate consequences for waywardness. If your children don't face consequences for their wrong actions today, then, one day, they (and society) will face the consequences of your failure. Satan wants your children. You go a long way toward giving them to him when you raise them without consequences.

I was still in Bible college when Jera and I had our first child. Among our best friends was another young married couple who had their first child about the same time. One day, Frank told me, "We've decided to raise our children without ever telling them 'No.' It's such a negative word."

This man was in *Bible college*! I asked, "Have you ever heard of, 'Thou shalt not commit adultery'? That's negative. In fact, our heavenly Father says no to lots of things."

My friend said, "Well, yeah, I guess I never thought about that."

Positive behavior merits praise. But for wrong behavior, there must be negative consequences. Scripture often talks about God disciplining us. Hebrews 12:11 says, "All discipline for the moment seems not to be joyful, but sorrowful; yet to those who have been trained by it, afterwards it yields the peaceful fruit of righteousness."

That's what we want for our children and for the world they will inhabit. Sadly, today we're seeing the results of a world where vast numbers of children have never known loving, consistent discipline. A couple of decades ago, you might go to a store and find the behavior of children appalling. Well, those children have grown up and now have children of their own. The problem has compounded.

You would not neglect a child's food or medical needs. You wouldn't let your child sleep on the streets. Such neglect would be egregious. So is the neglect of discipline.

Instruction

In English, we think of the word "instruction" as positive. But the Greek word used in Ephesians 6:4, *nouthesia*, carries both positive and negative connotations. It speaks of teaching with warnings. Proverbs 13:20 is a good example of this: "He who walks with wise men will be wise, but the companion of fools will suffer harm." Our children need this kind of instruction. They need to be told to pick their friends carefully. Their friends will move them toward God or away from God. The wrong crowd will get them in trouble (1 Corinthians 15:33), so they need to be wise.

The language of Ephesians 6:4 is intentional. Dads, train your children. Don't provoke them to anger. Don't leave them to figure stuff out alone. Don't abandon them in the most important areas of life. Instruct them. Train them. Discipline them. Teach them. When they go the wrong way, be consistent in giving them consequences.

One of my sons had a problem with anger when he was little. We memorized several proverbs together. When anger would begin to build in him, I would look at him and say, "What's your verse?" And he would give me a verse, like this one from Proverbs 29:11: "A fool always loses his temper, but a wise man holds it back."

Then I would ask, "What kind of man will you be?" and he would answer, "A wise man." Sometimes he would lose his temper, and there would be consequences. It was important that he face my mild consequences when he was young so that he would not face society's larger consequences for men out of control later in life.

"OF THE LORD"

What kind of discipline and instruction are we talking about? "Discipline and instruction *of the Lord.*" That is the key.

Your job as discipliner-in-chief will wane as the years pass. When your children reach adulthood, you won't be sending them to a corner or giving them a timeout. You will, I hope, always be a source of wisdom, but your job as teacher will wane. Your relationship will not end when they become adults. What will be left? What will your relationship be based on?

Through the years, I've talked with countless men who felt grateful for football or some other sport because it gave them something to talk about with their dads. I'm glad they share something in common, but it's also sad. When a man tells me that, I hear a deep loneliness in those words. When your sons and daughters are grown, if you want to have more in common with them than sports, start having more in common with them now.

There's no better way to do that than to develop a mutual interest in understanding the things of God. It all begins by being committed to instructing your children in the Lord.

TWELVE AREAS OF TRAINING

Here are 12 areas in which to train your children:

TRAIN YOUR CHILDREN

1. Show Them God's Wonders

When you interact with your children, as much as you possibly can, make sure they see the natural world Jesus made. While modern technology offers much that makes us marvel, it shows the glory of man, the engineering of man, and the wisdom of man. Don't get me wrong—technology can be amazing. But man's innovations pale when compared to the works of God.

Let me give an example. Matthew 24:1 says, "Jesus came out from the temple and was going away when His disciples came up to point out the temple buildings to Him." Herod the Great was responsible for refurbishing the temple over many years and turning it into a majestic structure. But he was a twisted, bloodthirsty man. And even though Herod's work on the temple was gorgeous, when you compare it with the creative work of the One who shaped the rings of Saturn, it's not that impressive.[1]

Psalm 111:2 says, "Great are the works of the Lord; they are studied by all who delight in them." Take your children into the wilderness. Give them binoculars or hiking sticks. Point to the earth, the water, and the sky. Say to them, "Look at what God created!" Delight together in God's creation. No human technology can compare. Give your children close encounters with the handiwork of the Lord.

2. Show Them God Moments

If you are a follower of Jesus Christ, then you have a story, a testimony. Do your kids know that story? Is Jesus working regularly in your life? Do your kids know that? I'm not talking about a religious moment. Rather, I am talking about faithfully passing on stories of your encounters with God to your sons and daughters—how you have walked with God and have seen His work in your life. How you have seen God answer prayer and how He has provided for you.

Deuteronomy 6:6-9 says,

> These words, which I am commanding you today, shall be on your heart. You shall teach them diligently to your sons and shall talk of them when you sit in your house and when you walk by the way and when you lie down and when you rise up. You shall bind them as a sign on your hand and they shall be as frontals on your forehead. You shall write them on the doorposts of your house and on your gates.

We assume our kids gather information about God on their own. But how can we know what they are learning unless we get involved with what they are learning? We should not leave the most important instruction of their lives solely to others or to what our children may (or may not) pick up from us.

What are your children learning from the words that pass through your lips? Ephesians 4:29 says, "Let no unwholesome word proceed from your mouth, but only such a word as is good for edification according to the need of the moment, so that it will give grace to those who hear." That includes the conversation in your own home. Psalm 119:46 says, "I will also speak of Your testimonies before kings and shall not be ashamed." If we can speak God's testimonies before kings, we can speak them before our kids.

The generation of Israel that left Egypt saw astounding miracles. They saw the Red Sea part. They saw fountains of water spring up in the desert. They ate manna from heaven. But before all this, they saw the plagues of Egypt and were there the night of the first Passover when death passed over their homes with doorframes covered in the blood of a lamb. God told the the people of Israel not only to remember these events, but to tell their children. In Deuteronomy 4:9, He said, "Give heed to yourself and keep your soul diligently, so that you do not forget the things which your eyes have seen and they do not depart from your heart all the days of your life; but make them known to your sons and your grandsons."

That's our job too! We're to make known the things of God to our children and our grandchildren. Do not leave them in the dark. Speak to them intentionally. Do not make assumptions about what they know. Be deliberate about giving them the light.

3. Make Jesus the Main Story

The death, burial, and resurrection of Jesus Christ should be at the heart of our everyday conversations as Christians. We may talk about a football game or a recent trip, but it's vital that our conversations focus on Jesus as well.

Remember the two disciples walking along the road to Emmaus? (Luke 24:13-35). They weren't talking about politics. Bigger things were afoot—they were despondent about Jesus' crucifixion. When Jesus joined them on their journey, they didn't realize at first who He was. But the conversation they had with this Beloved Stranger was all about Jesus. And then their eyes were opened…and they recognized the resurrected Jesus! Then He vanished from their sight.

As the two disciples returned to Jerusalem, they were so fired up that nothing could have diverted their conversation to lesser things. Jesus is still risen, and that fact still changes everything. It should fire us up too.

4. Call Them to Sacrifice

Children want to live for something bigger than themselves. Society teaches them that they are the center of everything, but in their hearts, they know there is more. And they long for it. They look at a world where personal gratification reigns supreme. They ask, "Is this all there is?"

Make sure your children understand that the gospel is not a hobby or a thing we indulge in briefly on Sunday mornings. Make sure they know that the calling of Jesus is on their whole life. They need to know that helping others is not meaningless. People have significance—and not just as a cause in a social movement. God made people in His own image, and God the Son laid down His life for them.

Do you feel a burden to help feed children in Africa? Let your kids help. There's a great deal they can do. Be creative. Find ways for them to join in, sacrificing their time and money for meaningful ministry. Make sure they feel part of the team. Enlarge their souls.

5. Teach Them to Seek the Lord's Direction in Ordinary Things

The Bible matters. It matters all the time and in every part of your children's lives. Prayer matters. Philippians 4:6 says, "Don't worry about anything; instead, pray about everything" (NLT). Does God say not to waste His time with the smaller concerns of life? No. His Word is clear. If something concerns you, pray about it. Even the ordinary matters to God. May your actions and words model and teach these truths to your children.

6. Help Them to Enjoy Jesus' Team

Broaden your children's horizons. Make sure they know that Team Jesus, the church, the body of Christ, is far bigger than just your immediate family, and it is their team. As followers of Jesus, we have family in every city in the world.

The problem comes when your children don't hear anything about Team Jesus. Or maybe worse, all they hear are your complaints. Satan is called the accuser of the Team (Revelation 12:10). Constant berating of fellow Christians plays right into Satan's hands. He wants to steal and kill and destroy, and do harm to your children. But Jesus "came that they may have life, and have it abundantly" (John 10:10).

Help your kids to enjoy Team Jesus and be excited about their teammates.

7. Teach Them to Delight in the Worship of Jesus

Worship is a 24/7 activity. First Corinthians 10:31 says, "Whether, then, you eat or drink or whatever you do, do all to the glory of God." Worship is "whatever you do," with the goal to honor God. Worship can occur through any godly attitudes, words, and actions.

Tell your children that obeying their parents with the right attitude is worshipping the Lord. Doing household chores, doing homework, and caring for their siblings can and should all be done with the spirit of worship—encourage them to do these things well in Jesus' name. Sadly, few Christians think or live this way. Help your children to make this a pattern early in their life. Anything less is robbing God of the glory He rightly deserves.

8. Help Them Embrace Jesus' Values

Children are unlikely to hear anything positive about the Ten Commandments in a public school. They don't know the enormous historical implications of those commandments, much less the even more enormous spiritual implications of them. Dads, we need to make up the difference at home. Help them memorize the Ten Commandments. Help your children to base their understanding of right and wrong, and truth and error, on God's eternal Word. Teach them to live out the commandments for Christ.

9. Model for Them the Practice of Surrendering to Jesus

Surrendering to Jesus involves repentance and confession to the Lord and to others, and that means reconciliation and restoration. In today's church are many who rarely or never confess their sins to God because they think everything is okay. Schools, songs, and television teach them to feel okay about themselves no matter what. It's easy to rationalize sin ("I did it because…"), compare sin ("At least I'm not as bad as so-and so!"), and go soft on sin (because, after all, God is a God of love and *is* love).

Your children need to understand the importance of kneeling before God in honesty and humility, saying, "I sinned!" and then presenting Him with specifics and asking Him for help toward change. That kind of surrender will empower them. It will keep the communication channels clear between themselves and God. And it will help them understand the power of confession in the healing of other relationships.

10. Help Them Live for the Honor of Jesus

Face it—your children will live for something. They will be all in and passionate about something. Help them to make that something be Jesus. Philippians 1:21 says, "To me, to live is Christ and to die is gain."

What a difference it makes when a child or adult realizes, *My life is bigger than me. My life belongs to Jesus.*

11. Remind Them That Jesus Cares

First Peter 5:7 says, "Casting all your care upon Him, for He cares for you" (NKJV).

Many Christian young people think of Jesus as an unhappy, unfriendly Lord who watches them to catch them if they make a mistake. They forget—or have never heard—that they can cast every one of their cares on Him because He loves them so much. We must teach them this comforting truth.

12. Expect Them to Live for Jesus' Calling

Expect your children to live for the glory of God. Some people say, "You can't put high expectations on children!" Increasingly, schools and society say we should lower our expectations of children. Self-proclaimed experts tell us to expect massive moral failure when young people reach high school.

Kids have a way of living down to, or up to, our expectations. Understand that they will not be perfect, but communicate to your kids that you expect good things. Stir within your children a desire and the motivation to live for Jesus' calling.

BUILD A LEGACY

I am here to say you can expect good things from your children and grandchildren. Teach them the Man Code at an age-appropriate level. Younger sons and grandsons may not be able to grasp the entire book, but they can grab hold of each of the main points. When each of our grandsons turned eight years old, Jera and I gave them a framed copy of the Man Code with a few photos of the boys with me and their dads (my son and son-in-law). They are part of a legacy of three generations of men who know and apply the Man Code! It's our gift to them, and we say, "This is how we expect you to live. Like real men. God expects it, and so do we." You might not have a three-generation legacy, but you can start right where you are. Let it start with YOU—start today!

Life together as a family can be a lot of fun! Raising children is one of the great pleasures of life. However, life is not a game. Proverbs 14:12 says, "There is a way which seems right to a man, but its end is the way of death." This world teaches kids that absolute truth doesn't exist and it changes over time, or that truth is subjective ("your truth is your truth, and my truth is my truth"). This relegates them to darkness and forces them to feel their way through life. We need to teach children that God has provided His immutable, eternal, powerful Word to be a light unto their feet so that they know how to go through life (Psalm 119:105).

Brother, get this right. Own it, live it, teach it to your children, and expect it to bear fruit in them. Be a good steward of your mind and your time by learning God's ways. Then be a good steward of that knowledge by living what you know and teaching it to your kids. Real men train their children.

27

NO CHILDREN?
THINK BIGGER

You may be asking, *What if I don't have children?* Great question!

PHYSICAL CHILDREN

I trusted Christ in my early teens. As I read the book of Proverbs over and over, I realized that God's wisdom helps the young man prepare for all the future phases of life: marriage, children, grand-children, etc. Tragically, many Christians today have embraced the folly of thinking solely about the present—one-dimensional living, if you will—and going through life one move at a time. I call that living like a checkers player.

But God wants us to think about the future. He calls us to be chess players. Look ahead and plan each move as you are guided by His wisdom. Chess players are always thinking four or five moves ahead. They also have a middle game plan and a closing plan. This is what wise men do in life. They are thinking ahead:

- What kind of woman should I marry? (see Proverbs 31).

223

- What kind of woman should I avoid? (see Proverbs 5 and 7).

- What should I do when I am tempted by anger and want to tell people off? (see Proverbs 12:16; 15:1; 16:32).

- What kind of friends should I make or avoid? (see Proverbs 1).

- What kind of children will I raise? (see Proverbs 14:6; 21:11; 28:26).

- What do I need to know to positively impact my grand-children? (see Proverbs 13:22).

God says those who have a godly plan have an advantage in life (see Proverbs 21:5; 22:3). Satan loves the naïve! That's why it's important to plan ahead. Even when I was too young to marry and too young for children or grandchildren, I started planning how I would raise any children or grandchildren God would entrust to me in the future.

God may bless you with your own biological children, He may bless you with a future wife who has children, or He may bless you with adopted children. He may bless you with all the above, so pre-pare now! Life is not a checkers game; it's a chess game.

SPIRITUAL CHILDREN

Scripture doesn't mention that the apostle Paul had any children, and we know he was single when penning the New Testament. How-ever, he did have a spiritual son—Timothy. He wrote these endear-ing words to him:

> To Timothy, my beloved son: Grace, mercy and peace from God the Father and Christ Jesus our Lord. I thank God, whom I serve with a clear conscience the way my forefathers did, as I constantly remember you in my prayers

night and day, longing to see you, even as I recall your
tears, so that I may be filled with joy (2 Timothy 1:2-4).

Paul met and invited Timothy along during his second missionary journey, recorded in Acts 16. Timothy was a young man with a
wonderful mother and grandmother who had taught him the Scriptures. His birth father was a Greek, apparently unsaved, and, as best
we can tell, he had abandoned the family. Paul took this young man
under his wing, and doing that changed the world!

Like Timothy, when I was a young man, I had several great men
of God take me under their wing. They left godly impressions on my
life, and as a result, I view them as my spiritual fathers. I pray that
my service to the Lord today delights and encourages them.

Brother, find some spiritual children! Invest in the younger men
whom God brings into your life. You will find them in your church,
your extended family, your workplace, or your neighborhood. Train
them in the things of God. Show them how real men live and die.

My hope is that God will grant you many spiritual children. The
apostle John had many such children, and he wrote these powerful
words to them: "I have no greater joy than this, to hear of my [spir-
itual] children walking in the truth" (3 John 4).

Real men train their children!

STUDY QUESTIONS

1. Have you personally shared the gospel of Jesus Christ with your children? Why or why not? Have you asked them to put their faith in Jesus? What is holding you back?

2. Are your children closer to God because of you, or are they further away from Him? Explain. How can you help them grow closer to God?

3. You cannot teach passion for Christ if you do not have it. On a scale of 1 to 10, how is your passion for Jesus? What number would your family, spouse, or children give you? Be real about this. How does that number make you feel? What can you do today to raise the bar?

4. Can your children recite the Ten Commandments? Can they think through life situations on TV, at school, at play, and apply their meaning? Why or why not? What can you do to help them?

5. If you have children, print out the 12 priorities that comprise the Man Code and start memorizing them together.

(You'll find the list near the end of the introduction of this book and at the end of this book.) Make the Man Code part of your regular vocabulary. Both your sons and daughters need it.

6. If you have no children:

   a. How are you preparing now for the children God may give you in the future? How will you train them to love Jesus, the gospel, the people of God? What will you teach them about ethics, sexuality, marriage, finances, tithing, investing, sharing, or serving? How will you discipline them? What tools do you need to start gathering, and what skills do you need to develop to do a good job?

   b. Who is your spiritual father? Who led you to Christ? Who gave you your first Bible? Who helped you learn your first verse?

   c. Who have you led to Christ? Who are you picking up and bringing to church or a Bible camp or a men's retreat? If you don't have spiritual children today, will you regret it in the future? What is holding you back? Be honest.

PART 11

REAL MEN DO NOT ABANDON THEIR FAMILIES

The pain of divorce or abandonment touches everyone at some time in some way. We must face it in the light of Scripture. Marriage vows are real. Because we take them before God, we must take them seriously. Promises made on our wedding day should never be taken lightly. Real men keep their promises of faithfulness to their wives and their children. Our faithful God never abandons us, and He calls us to be like Him.

As a side note, we commonly think of a man abandoning his family only when the couple have children. But even if you are childless, you have a family. You and your wife are a family. Abandon her, and you are abandoning your family.

The Lord loves justice and does not forsake His godly ones; they are preserved forever, but the descendants of the wicked will be cut off.

PSALM 37:28

When you make a vow to God, do not be late in paying it; for He takes no delight in fools. Pay what you vow! It is better that you should not vow than that you should vow and not pay.

ECCLESIASTES 5:4-5

Men with good intentions make promises.
Men with good character keep them.[1]
RONALD OLIVER

28

LEAVE NO ONE BEHIND

The US Army has a special team of soldiers: the long-range reconnaissance patrol, or the LRRP teams (pronounced *lurp*). These teams go behind enemy lines. They infiltrate the enemy's backyard, learn what is going on, and report it to command. In Vietnam, LRRPs such as Tiger Force made it their job to "outguerrilla the guerrillas."

These guys go through infamously difficult training. They work together in severe and dangerous conditions. LRRP teams become extremely committed to one another. They live by the code "LRRPs don't leave LRRPs." It doesn't matter what happens out there. None of them will be left behind. None will be forgotten. Each one commits his life to this code.

God calls men to that kind of commitment in marriage. Real men do not leave their spouses.

Not everyone wants to hear this—especially those who have already gone through divorce and don't want to relive the pain. Believe me, pastors who have done counseling are acutely aware of that pain.

Oddly, the person who feels the most pain and guilt over a divorce is often the one who did the least to cause the divorce.

For many, the source of that pain continues to wreak havoc after the divorce. And while pastors don't like to cause a person to feel pain, if we're able to talk about it, we can help the pain to subside—and we can help others to avoid the pain.

Meanwhile, we must move forward. How? Confess the past, forsake the past, and go forward in Jesus' name.

CAUGHT IN THE ACT

John 8 tells about Jesus arriving at the temple in Jerusalem early one morning. People saw Him, gathered around Him, and He began to teach. Some commotion interrupted Him. A group of religious leaders brought a woman forward and threw her down at the Lord's feet. " 'Teacher,' they said to Jesus, 'this woman was caught in the act of adultery. The law of Moses says to stone her. What do you say?' " (verses 4-5 NLT).

This was not about the woman. She was a mere pawn in the hands of evil men. This was an attack on Jesus, a trap. If He said not to stone her, He would seem to be contradicting God's law (Leviticus 20:10). If He said to stone her, He would be breaking Roman law (John 18:31).

But to Jesus, there was a bigger picture: the glory of God, the law, forgiveness, redemption, *and* the woman. He saw her as a real and needy person—a person being humiliated by her sin and terrorized by her accusers. She needed redemption and redirection in life.

There is an interesting omission in the religious leaders' announcement to Jesus. Where was the man? The leaders testified that the "woman was caught in the act of adultery" (verse 4). If caught in the act, shouldn't someone else have also been caught with her?

Make no mistake: The Bible condemns adultery. To protect society from this evil, the law of Moses commanded the death penalty for those who committed it. This was no casual sin. It's not recreational or victimless. Its penalty was literal, but also symbolic. Adultery kills. It kills marriages, families, futures, peace, and joy. We cannot quantify the harm done by this sin. It includes anguish, sadness, rebellion, anger, loss of productivity, disorder, and more. The pain from it ripples out across society and causes harm in ways both small and large.

But Jesus did not stone the woman. Neither did He order His followers to stone her. He did not physically or verbally slap her around. He knelt and began to write in the dirt. I imagine the woman nearby on the ground, weeping in shame and fear. She sees Jesus stop His writing, and she wonders what He will order done to her.

THE FINGER WITH WHICH HE WROTE

We don't know what Jesus wrote. Many have speculated, but we don't know. Some say He wrote about the accusers, perhaps names and the dates of their own indiscretions. If I were to guess, I think it might have been from the Ten Commandments:

- You shall have no other gods.

- You shall have no idols.

- You shall not take God's name in vain.

- You shall keep the Sabbath holy.

If my speculation seems strange, consider the most important fact about this situation. The most important fact is not *what Jesus wrote*, but *who Jesus is*. Whose finger wrote in the dirt that day, and whose finger carved those words in stone on Mount Sinai so long ago? The finger of God carved the Ten Commandments, and the finger of God wrote in the dirt on the Temple Mount.

Finally, Jesus stood up. He turned to the woman's accusers and said, "He who is without sin among you, let him be the first to throw a stone at her" (verse 7).

After saying this, Jesus knelt back to the ground and wrote more in the dirt. Perhaps He wrote:

- You shall honor your father and mother.

- You shall not murder.

- You shall not commit adultery.

- You shall not steal.

- You shall not lie.

- You shall not covet.

Lie? Covet? The teachers knew the law. Even in their pride, they knew that as surely as this woman had committed the sin of adultery, they had committed the sins of covetousness and lying. Each of them, just like her, stood guilty in the sight of God.

If the woman had been paying careful attention, she might have heard footsteps shuffling behind her—beginning nearby, then growing fainter. For the moment at least, the words of Jesus stopped their virtue signaling, their religious fervor, their rage, and their bloodlust.

"When Jesus had raised Himself up and saw no one but the woman, He said to her, 'Woman, where are those accusers of yours? Has no one condemned you?' She said, 'No one, Lord.' And Jesus said to her, 'Neither do I condemn you; go and sin no more'" (John 8:10-11 NKJV).

Jesus gave the perfect answer at every point in the story—responses worthy of the Son of God. He confronted the sinful pride of those who set this trap for Him. He showed mercy to the woman, while loving her enough to command her to live godly. He contradicted neither the law of Moses nor of Rome. He taught everyone an unforgettable lesson, while shaming the self-righteous. Finally, His statement did not preclude a future when He will judge. Even by the high standard of "he who is without sin" (John 8:7), Jesus can judge because He is without sin.

"THANKS BE TO GOD THROUGH JESUS CHRIST OUR LORD!"

Jesus will judge the world (Acts 17:31), but that was not the purpose of His first coming. He explained in John 3:17-18, "God did not send the Son into the world to judge the world, but that the world might be saved through Him. He who believes in Him is not judged; he who does not believe has been judged already, because he has not believed in the name of the only begotten Son of God."

Today Jesus saves, heals, and redeems (1 Peter 3:18). First John 2:2 says, "He Himself is the propitiation for our sins." That means He sacrificed His life as the atonement for our sins. When we accept that provision for our redemption, we are born again in Christ (John 3:3). We still sometimes sin, but His clear, concise instruction to us remains: "Go and sin no more."

God gave Paul an amazing understanding of many truths, yet Paul still failed. Romans 7:14-25 expresses the lament of every Christian who fights pride, selfishness, or covetousness—and sometimes loses a battle. Verse 19 says, "The good that I want, I do not do, but I practice the very evil that I do not want." Verse 24 says, "Wretched man that I am! Who will set me free from the body of this death?"

Then in Romans 7:25–8:1 comes the glorious answer: "Thanks be to God through Jesus Christ our Lord! So then, on the one hand I myself with my mind am serving the law of God, but on the other, with my flesh the law of sin. Therefore there is now no condemnation for those who are in Christ Jesus."

Maybe you have gone through a divorce. Maybe it was your fault, or maybe not. Either way, you probably struggled with guilt. If you have confessed your sin and turned from it, but find yourself still struggling with guilt, remember the words of Jesus to the woman caught in adultery: "Neither do I condemn you; go and sin no more" (John 8:11 NKJV).

"There is now no condemnation for those who are in Christ Jesus"! Are you in Christ Jesus? Then God no longer condemns you. Are you determined to have a higher standard than God? I assure you that you cannot. So stop condemning yourself.

That said, let's see if we can help prevent others from that same pain.

29

DIVORCE

Despite what you may have heard, the divorce rate among Christians is not as high as it is in society at large. Don't look at the statistics on people who claim to be Christian. Narrow down the count to people who exhibit basic Christian behavior. For instance, do they attend church on a relatively regular basis? In *Christians Are Hate-Filled Hypocrites...and Other Lies You've Been Told*, sociologist Bradley Wright explains that among people who identify as Christians but rarely attend church, 60 percent have been divorced. But among regular churchgoers, that number falls to 38 percent.[1]

That's still too high. It's still a symptom of a church that too often reflects the culture rather than standing apart from it. We shouldn't do only a little better with our marriages. We should do much better.

God calls us to stand for something greater. For me, this is real. It is sensitive, and it is raw. As I grew up, my family relationships required frequent realignments. Imagine an uncle who leaves his wife. Suddenly, certain cousins no longer attend family gatherings. A new aunt shows up, and she's not alone. She brings in her kids. Your aunt who was left behind brings a new uncle with his kids into the family fold too. It all becomes very complex. Instead of visiting two sets of grandparents (four people), now you're visiting four sets (eight people). Things get tense at big family functions when everyone is invited. Relational connectivity—so important in life—degrades. So does your investment in people. This is serious!

God is not a cosmic killjoy. He loves people. He works to protect His name and to protect us from foolishness. Have you ever been told *not* to do something, done it anyway, then found out you should have paid attention? Listen carefully to God from the start, and you can avoid many painful regrets.

THE VOW

Marriage centers on a vow—not just a vow to a woman, but a vow before God. Remember that 1 Peter 3:7 tells husbands to "honor" their wives "so that your prayers will not be hindered."

Malachi 2:13-14 carries a similar thought. In these verses, God says to unfaithful men,

> You cover the altar of the LORD with tears, with weeping and with groaning, because He no longer regards the offering or accepts it with favor from your hand. Yet you say, "For what reason?" Because the LORD has been a witness between you and the wife of your youth, against whom you have dealt treacherously, though she is your companion and your wife by covenant.

Once again, we see a link between how a man treats his wife, and the way God chooses to answer his prayers.

In Malachi, God laments that men make promises to women in their youth, but later decide to trade in the older model for a newer one. When a woman is at the peak of her attractiveness from a worldly viewpoint, the man promises to love her, nurture her, care for her, and protect her. A few years later, the man notices that an attractive younger woman treats him like he's smart, funny, and handsome—and he likes it. He decides to dump the "wife of [his] youth" in favor of someone new.

Through the prophet Malachi, God said, in effect, that every marriage is a big deal. Verse 14 reads, "The LORD has been a witness between you and the wife of your youth." God heard the vow. When you made that vow in His presence, it became binding on you.

Too often, weddings have become occasions with which to impress friends and relatives. They have become a game of who spends the most money, has the biggest cake, finds the coolest venue, or travels to the most extravagant destination. Weddings have become an excuse for a party...or worse.

But God is the primary witness at any wedding. May we have weddings that we can enjoy together with Him. May we have weddings that celebrate marriage as God sees marriage. He is the primary witness, and if you break your vows, you answer to Him.

'TIL DEATH DO US PART

Malachi 2:14 says, "The LORD has been a witness between you and the wife of your youth, against whom you have dealt treacherously." *Treachery* means betrayal. It means unfaithfulness, the breaking of a solemn vow.

Couples today often make clever alterations to their vows. For example, they will change "as long as we both shall live" to "as long as we both shall love." Insightful as that may sound, it doesn't get you off the hook with God. He designed marriage for life —'til death do us part.

Unmarried women reading this book should think about this. If your fiancé wants your vows to say something like, "I promise to love you as long as our hearts are mutually bound," you may have a serious problem. Do not marry a man who seeks to diminish the commitment called for in a vow! An empty vow like that means as soon as he no longer feels warm and fuzzy toward you, it's over, and he will be gone. (By the way, this applies to you as well, if that's how you want to revise your vows.)

If you get sick and he has to take care of you, Mr. As-long-as-we-both-have-nothing-but-great-feelings-about-each-other will be gone. He will be out of there. This is a man who wants to enjoy what you can offer now, including sex, but if your health happens to fail, he's going to run. You want to find a man who will stand by you in sickness and in health. You want a real man—God's kind of man!

The best-known English-language marriage vows were first published in *The Book of Common Prayer*: "…to have and to hold from this day forward, for better for worse, for richer for poorer, in sickness and in health, to love and to cherish, till death us do part, according to God's holy ordinance."

These vows are Bible-based.[2]

In Malachi 2:14, God calls your wife "your companion." A companion is a friend. If your wife is not your friend, then you have work to do. Choose to make her your friend. A companion is also a fellow traveler, someone who goes through the difficulties and dangers of life with you. When the locusts ate the crops, she was there, fighting and scrapping with you. When the fire took your home, it took her stuff too. When the investment went bad or the job ended, she tightened the purse strings, and together you carried on.

This is why Proverbs 18:22 says, "He who finds a wife finds a good thing"!

From the beginning, God knew that man would need a special companion. In Genesis 2:18, God says, "It is not good for the man to be alone; I will make him a helper."

DO NOT DEAL TREACHEROUSLY

Would you now deal treacherously with that companion, that helper, that person to whom you made vows before Almighty God?

As I write these things, I can imagine someone saying, "Yes, but…" Maybe you are thinking, *Yes, but she does things that make me crazy. She intentionally infuriates me. She's always nagging me. She spends money like it's going out of style. Every time I feel romantic, she gets a headache. She gets meaner every year. She doesn't like me anymore. She is the worst companion on the planet. She doesn't like anything I enjoy. It's tough.*

Even if you are right on every count, another "Yes, but…" should concern you more: "Yes, but…I made a covenant before God."

Deuteronomy 23:21 says, "When you make a vow to the LORD your God, you shall not delay to pay it, for it would be sin in you, and the LORD your God will surely require it of you."

The next verse gives the obvious alternative: "However, if you refrain from vowing, it would not be sin in you." That's important. Going on a date is not the same as saying, "Till death us do part." Be careful about who you make a vow to and with. Verse 23 says, "You shall be careful to perform what goes out from your lips, just as you have voluntarily vowed to the LORD your God, what you have promised."

Ecclesiastes 5:5 says it simply: "It is better that you should not vow than that you should vow and not pay."

If you don't want to keep the vow, don't get married. But once you get married, God is a witness to that vow, and He takes it seriously.

DIVORCE IS A SPIRITUAL ISSUE

What is the answer to the seriousness of the marriage vows and living them out? Of refusing to abandon your family? The passage we've been reading in Malachi twice tells us to take heed to our spirits. In Malachi 2:15-16, God says, "'Take heed then to your spirit, and let no one deal treacherously against the wife of your youth. For I hate divorce,' says the LORD, the God of Israel, 'and him who covers his garment with wrong,' says the LORD of hosts. 'So take heed to your spirit, that you do not deal treacherously.'"

Understand the spiritual dimension here: "Take heed to your spirit." When a man abandons his family, it is a spiritual issue.

In Malachi 2:16, God says, "I hate divorce." When God hates something, we should pay special attention. Hate is a strong emotion. It goes to the heart. God's powerful expression of emotion here should make us sit up and take notice. This does not mean that God hates people who have gone through a divorce. Some of those who hate divorce the most, hate it because of their own experience with it.

Why does God use such strong terms? Because He detests lying, betrayal, and unfaithfulness. He delights in truth and loyalty. His joy is to see you win against sin and know His blessing. God hates divorce because He loves us. He sees the ripples of pain that emanate from divorce, ripples that can go on for generations. God hates divorce because He loves children, and He loves their parents.

Finally, this passage brings us back to the theme. Verse 16 says, "Take heed to your spirit, that you do not deal treacherously."

If you are married, you made a vow. Be faithful to your God. This is a spiritual issue. After having worked with hundreds of couples, I can assure you that if you endure and work on the problems of today, you will be happier in two years than if you had gotten divorced.

30

"WHAT GOD HAS JOINED TOGETHER"

Pastor Mark, you don't understand. I have rights!" I hear those words often. I know you have rights. But you need to put those rights into context.

The Pharisees tried repeatedly to trick Jesus into saying something they could use against Him. In Matthew 19, they broached the topic of divorce. They probably asked their question believing that if you want to get a religious leader to offend one group or another, get him talking about divorce. Matthew 19:3 reports what happened: "Some Pharisees came to Jesus, testing Him and asking, 'Is it lawful for a man to divorce his wife for any reason at all?'"

Divorce was a hot topic in those days. Some said you could get rid of your wife for burning a bagel. Others found this notion abominable. It boiled down to a matter of rights. They wanted Jesus to define a man's rights regarding divorce.

The Lord began His answer with a question: "Have you not read…?" (verse 4). He asks if they have looked in the Scriptures. He says the same to us as well: "Have you not read? What does the Bible say?"

FROM THE BEGINNING

The Lord said, "Have you not read that He who created them from the beginning made them male and female, and said, 'For this reason a man shall leave his father and mother and shall be joined to his wife, and the two shall become one flesh'?" (verses 4-5).

Does Jesus believe the Bible? Yes, He does! That's why He constantly pointed people to it, as He did here. After quoting the passage, Jesus gave His commentary on it. He began, "So they are no longer two, but one flesh" (verse 6).

This statement takes us back to Genesis. How could two become one? A merely human institution could not accomplish this. Marriage is the work of God. He binds you together. The second half of verse 6 gives us the kicker: "What therefore God has joined together, let no man separate."

Doctors cannot separate conjoined twins who share one heart. Marriage is supposed to be like that. At marriage, God creates something that did not exist before. That which He binds together should not be separated. When a marriage is separated, it will be painful and even debilitating to the individuals involved.

SPECIFIC INSTRUCTIONS
REGARDING MARRIAGE

People sometimes say to me, "The Bible is ambiguous." These people have not read it. When we read the Bible, we find specific action points, such as those in 1 Corinthians 7:1-17. These are not just generic directions; they are highly specific. We won't look at all of them, but let's go through some key ones.

Verses 1 through 7 describe how the marriage relationship should work. In Corinth, some taught that celibacy in marriage made you more spiritual. That may sound ethereal or saintly, but it is wrong. Look at verse 5: "Stop depriving one another, except by agreement for a time, so that you may devote yourselves to prayer, and come together again so that Satan will not tempt you because of your lack of self-control."

I cannot tell you how many times over the past 30 years someone has come to me saying, "I pushed my spouse into the arms of another person." This is not an excuse for the person who cheats. This is a warning. Do not test your spouse's resolve by depriving him or her of marital sex.[1]

In verse 8, Paul recommends that the unmarried and widows should not seek marriage. Verse 9 then acknowledges that will not work for everyone. "If they do not have self-control, let them marry; for it is better to marry than to burn with passion."

Verses 10-11 say, "To the married I give instructions, not I, but the Lord [referring to Jesus in Matthew 19], that the wife should not leave her husband (but if she does leave, let her remain unmarried, or else be reconciled to her husband), and that the husband should not divorce his wife."

What does this mean? Keep the vows! Do not abandon your wife. If you are both believers in Christ and are married, you made a vow before God, and God takes it seriously. You don't have "rights" to do whatever you want. You have the duty and obligation to follow the living God and honor Him. Obedience to God trumps rights!

Maybe you became a believer after you were married, and your spouse is still an unbeliever. Look at verses 12-13:

> To the rest I say, not the Lord [meaning Jesus did not
> give specific instructions on this], that if any brother has
> a wife who is an unbeliever, and she consents to live with
> him, he must not divorce her. And a woman who has an
> unbelieving husband, and he consents to live with her,
> she must not send her husband away.

God's priority remains the preservation of marriage. If you are single and considering marriage, do not marry someone who is looking for an exception clause. Still, it is important to know that the New Testament does give two such clauses—adultery and abandonment.

In every case, may our priorities align with God's. Real men do not abandon their families. They do not leave their wives. They do not leave their children.

OBSERVATIONS

First, why is God so emphatic on this issue? Because He is faithful. God does not break His promises. His words reflect His perfect character. God is not looking for a way to get rid of you or ditch you. His insistence about keeping marriage vows reflects His character. You cannot change the past. Find the path from here forward that honors Jesus.

Second, what if I come from a family where divorce was common? Friends often tell me, "We have an ongoing cycle of divorce in our family." That was true for my family as well. But I said to myself, "Enough! I want to follow Jesus and, with His help, stop this cycle now." Jera and I have been married 35 years. God is big enough to break any cycle!

Third, marry well! Relationships are complex and people change with time. Tell your children, your grandchildren, your neighbors, and your friends, "Marry well." Do not marry someone without a lot of careful thought. Do not marry someone who isn't serious about the vows. And do not marry someone with the idea you can change them. The chances are too great they will never change.

God hates divorce, but this is a sinful world. People sometimes end up getting divorced even when they don't want to. But in His grace and kindness, God gives clear direction and a straight path. Real men do not abandon their families; they do not leave their wives and their children.

STUDY QUESTIONS

1. How have you personally been hurt by divorce or dysfunction in your family? Who will break the cycle? How can you do marriage and family better than what you experienced as a child?

2. When was the last time you reflected on your wedding vows? Is it time to formally (or informally) renew them with your wife? How is your commitment to God?

3. Anyone can leave a family. Anyone can run away. Anyone can destroy a marriage. How will you preserve, protect, and build yours? What are your next three steps?

PART 12:

REAL MEN LOVE THE GOSPEL AND THE CHURCH

Devotion to the church begins by loving the gospel, the good news of God's redemptive plan through His only begotten Son, Jesus Christ. The church is not a building, but a people called and set apart by God to be the body of Christ. It exists as a local entity and a global one.

I am not ashamed of the gospel, for it is the power of God for salvation to everyone who believes.
ROMANS 1:16

I will build My church; and the gates of Hades will not overpower it.
MATTHEW 16:18

You have one business on earth—to save souls.
JOHN WESLEY

The one indispensable requirement for producing godly, mature Christians is godly, mature Christians.[1]
KEVIN DEYOUNG

31

GO BIG
OR GO HOME

The gospel is *timeless*; it is for every nation, every generation, every phase of life. One hundred years from now, it will still be needed as much as we need it today. There will never be a time in human history when it will not be in demand.

The gospel is *meaningful*. Unlike so much of what we do in life that has no meaning, the gospel that we believe and share takes spiritually dead people and makes them alive. It is the gold standard of all that is significant.

The gospel is *noble*. No warrior has found a more glorious cause to live for, sacrifice for, and die for. The gospel is everything weighty for real men. You see this in Jesus' life, the apostles' lives, and godly men throughout history.

THE GOSPEL IS CERTAIN

We all like a sure bet, a sure win, a sure victory. Yet experience tells us that most seemingly sure things are not so sure. In fact, when someone promises a sure thing, you can be assured it is *not* sure! Unless, of course, it is Jesus, the Son of God. Read His words:

> Truly, truly, I say to you, unless one is born again, he cannot see the kingdom of God (John 3:3).

> Truly, truly, I say to you, he who hears My word, and believes Him who sent Me, has eternal life, and does not come into judgment, but has passed out of death into life (John 5:24).

> Truly, truly, I say to you, he who believes has eternal life (John 6:47).

The gospel of Jesus Christ is the one thing on which you can bet your life! It is the one thing on which you can invest your life without any regrets. It is the one thing that brings all the blessings of God to bear in our lives and the lives of those whom we care about. It is *that* certain.

THE GOSPEL IS MISSIONAL

You feel the passion in your soul. You need to live for something that is meaningful, timeless, and noble. Nothing is worse than seeing a man who has invested his life only to feel (and know) that, at the end, "What I did was for nothing!" I have heard and seen hundreds of times, "Mark, I wasted my life!"

Whatever your God-given gifts, education, opportunities, financial holdings, career, or season of life, Jesus is calling you to get on mission. Doing this will take guts. It will take sacrifice. It will be demanding. And it will also be glorious and eternal. Jesus is clear on your mission.

Go into all the world and preach the gospel to all creation (Mark 16:15).

Go therefore and make disciples of all the nations, baptizing them in the name of the Father and the Son and the Holy Spirit, teaching them to observe all that I commanded you; and lo, I am with you always, even to the end of the age (Matthew 28:19-20).

You will receive power when the Holy Spirit has come upon you; and you shall be My witnesses both in Jerusalem, and in all Judea and Samaria, and even to the remotest part of the earth (Acts 1:8).

Don't waste your life. This is your mission. It has greater implications than any military mission in history. It supersedes and outperforms any business model on the planet. Jesus is calling you up. He wants you deployed for action. Why love the gospel of Jesus? It is your mission.

THE GOSPEL IS POWERFUL

We love powerful things: planes, trucks, cars, tractors, business, people, etc. Do you want to see real power? It is in the gospel of Jesus Christ. Read what God's Word says: "I am not ashamed of the gospel, for it is the power of God for salvation to everyone who believes, to the Jew first and also to the Greek" (Romans 1:16).

The gospel is so powerful it unleashes God's grace to save people. Whatever their nationality, skin tone, language, generation, and economic or social setting, the gospel can make someone a child of God, a citizen of heaven, a person for God's own possession. No government, business, or any other created thing has such power. It does not exist.

Many times, people have said to me, "Mark, God would never accept me. He could never forgive me for what I have done." Perhaps you are feeling this way right now. Know this: The power of Jesus is greater than the power of sin! That why the Bible says,

> Do not be deceived; neither fornicators, nor idolaters, nor adulterers, nor effeminate, nor homosexuals, nor thieves, nor the covetous, nor drunkards, nor revilers, nor swindlers, will inherit the kingdom of God. Such were some of you; but you were washed, but you were sanctified, but you were justified in the name of the Lord Jesus Christ and in the Spirit of our God (1 Corinthians 6:9-11).

Why love the gospel of Jesus? It is powerful.

THE GOSPEL IS CLEAR

A couple years ago, I met a man, and we started talking. He was sharp, well-dressed, intelligent, well-educated, and thoughtful. Being on mission, I eventually introduced the gospel into our conversation, saying that Jesus, the Son of God, came and died on the cross and rose the third day. I invited him to trust in Jesus alone so that he might have everlasting life and be in a right relationship with God. He looked at me in shock and said, "It cannot be that simple."

Brother, the gospel is complex in its execution. The Creator became flesh. Theologians call it the hypostatic union. I could go on, but suffice it to say, it's complicated. However, what about the part we need to understand and communicate to help folks join the family of God? Well, it's simple and clear:

1. *Sin separates us from the living God.* We have all broken the Ten Commandments and are morally guilty before God. The consequence is hell—eternity apart from God.

   • "All have sinned and fall short of the glory of God" (Romans 3:23).

   • "The wages of sin is death, but the free gift of God is eternal life in Christ Jesus our Lord" (Romans 6:23).

2. *God is good. He has a plan to restore us to Himself and give us the gift of eternal life.* Jesus is the Savior that God promised and provided. He became man, lived a sinless life, died on the cross to pay for the our sins, and God raised Him on the third day.

   • "He [God] made Him [Jesus] who knew no sin to be sin on our behalf, so that we might become the righteousness of God in Him" (2 Corinthians 5:21).

   • "I make known to you, brethren, the gospel which I preached to you, which also you received, in which also you stand, by which also you are saved...For I delivered to you as of first importance what I also received, that Christ died for our sins according to the Scriptures, and that He was buried, and that He was raised on the third day according to the Scriptures" (1 Corinthians 15:1-4).

   • "God demonstrates His own love toward us, in that while we were yet sinners, Christ died for us" (Romans 5:8).

3. *Each of us needs to respond to Jesus and His work on the cross.* God's gift of salvation comes to us the moment we *repent* (that is, we change our mind about our sin and trust

Jesus' work on the cross alone to save us from our sin) and *believe* (we trust/rely) in Him alone to make us right with God. This is an individual decision between you and the Lord.

- "By grace you have been saved through faith; and that not of yourselves, it is the gift of God; not as a result of works, so that no one may boast" (Ephesians 2:8-9).

- "As many as received Him, to them He gave the right to become children of God, even to those who believe in His name" (John 1:12).

- "He who has the Son has the life; he who does not have the Son of God does not have the life. These things I have written to you who believe in the name of the Son of God, so that you may know that you have eternal life" (1 John 5:12-13).

Saving faith includes three elements:

1. *Knowledge* of who Jesus is and what He did on the cross;

2. *mental assent* as to the reality of His work in history;

3. and lastly, *to trust in Him alone* to make you right with God.

When all three elements unite, we have saving faith.

A wise man once said it this way: "It is *history* when I say, 'Jesus died.' It is *theology* when I say, 'Jesus died for sin.' It is *salvation* when I say, 'Jesus died for my sin.'"

The Bible records a gospel event in Acts 16, when two Christian men, Paul and Silas, were imprisoned for helping a slave girl. She was demon-possessed, and they had cast the demon out through the power of Christ. They were put in jail for doing good, not evil. Throughout the night, they shared about Jesus and sang praises to Him.

In the middle of the night, a great earthquake destroyed the prison, creating an opportunity for Paul and Silas to escape. The warden, knowing the Roman penalty of death for losing prisoners, pulled out his sword and was about to commit suicide. These two Christians called out in the darkness, "Stop, we are still here!" Shaking in unbelief that these two men had not run for their lives, he went to them and asked, "Sirs, what must I do to be saved?" They said, "Believe in the Lord Jesus, and you will be saved, you and your household" (Acts 16:30-31).

If you have not put your trust in Jesus Christ alone to make you acceptable to God, *now is the time*. Do not resist God! If you feel the Holy Spirit stirring your heart right now, then believe in the Lord Jesus Christ, and you will be saved. Do you know your sin has separated you from God? Do you know that Jesus died on the cross as God's *only provision* to pay for your sin? Do you right now trust in Jesus and His work alone to save you? If so, express your faith in Him in prayer: "Lord, I know my sin has separated me from You and ensures my place in hell. Thank You for sending Jesus to die on the cross to pay for sin, my sin, and take the wrath I deserve. I trust in Him alone to save me right now, the best I know how. Save me, Lord, in Jesus' name."

If you have prayed those words, welcome to the family of God! You now have the Holy Spirit of God in you to help you, comfort you, and enlighten you.

Belief in God is more than lip service; it's a matter of the heart. God will not be tricked or mocked. If you truly have placed your complete trust in Christ, the Holy Spirit will begin to change your life. He will draw you to the things of God. Saving faith always bears itself out in life. Not perfectly, but over time. Godliness is a growth process, and it begins when you realize you are a sinner and Jesus died to pay for your sin.

Why do real men love the gospel? It is truly timeless. It is dripping with real meaning. And it is so noble that it demands our lives. It is that simple and that clear.

32

STICK WITH THE PLAN

Satan hates the church. Jesus loves the church. Whose side are you on?

The church, in many places, has been under all kinds of attacks in recent years. Christian enclaves with history going back to ancient times have been obliterated. In Europe, some portions of the Bible have become illegal to read in public. During the COVID-19 pandemic, what began as a 14-day lockdown of everything, including churches, became an ongoing battle for the future and soul of the church.

If the church was not precious to you before COVID-19, it should be now. Different forces at work in the world today would destroy the church, if it were possible. They are using every means at their disposal. In some cases, they may succeed in destroying certain legal entities that we call churches, and they may destroy or repurpose buildings that are often called churches. But the gates of hell will not prevail against the real church of Jesus Christ!

Jesus calls each of us, as members of the church, to defend the timeless truths of His Word (1 Peter 3:15).

CHURCH MEN

One of the great blessings of my life is that, early in my walk with Christ, God put me in a great church. The leadership loved and taught the Bible. The people loved and taught me. Because of that, my church life became a wonderful adventure.

I am a visual learner. So I needed models and examples. Certain men in that church allowed me to see Christ in action through them.

There was an older man who is with Jesus now, Ben Peek. I would ride my bike to church early in the morning, and Ben would already be there. He would be setting up for a communion service or making sure the ushers had their instructions. Under his leadership, the deacons would come forward with the communion elements. They stood tall like West Point cadets as they prepared to serve the Lord's table to 1,500 people. They focused on Ben. At his signal, they moved in unison, serving the people of God. Ben loved his church family.

Jesse, 20 years my senior, owned and managed a family ranch. He drove a four-wheel-drive truck and often pulled a horse trailer, and in that trailer, he transported horses. I loved it! Jesse led actual cattle drives, moving cows up onto a mountain. "Head 'em up; move 'em out!"—just like in the old cowboy movies. Jesse was a real cowboy, and that impressed me. He was fun, boisterous, and radiated with life. As busy as Jesse was on the ranch, he made time for heavy involvement in church. He led the singing, Bible studies, and leadership meetings. He ran a time-intensive business, and he must have gotten tired. But he loved the church.

Frank owned a construction company and was well known throughout the region. When a building project arose at church, Frank got it done. The size and complexity of the job did not matter. Big or small, he could handle it. He used his skill set to advance the gospel.

Frank was a servant-leader. I watched him give of himself tirelessly and at great personal cost. He loved the church.

Nick served as one of our deacons. He also served as a colonel in the US Air Force. We lived near March Air Force Base, a Strategic Air Command base during the Cold War. He was one of a number of B-52 bomber pilots who helped keep our nation safe—an amazing guy! Every Sunday, he and his family were in church. He taught Bible classes of all kinds, served as chair of the leadership team, and trained younger leaders. He was a man of the Word and a man of the church.

Dan was a white-collar professional with a heart for the mountains. He loved fishing the small creeks of the Sierra Nevada mountains. He was a quiet, wise, and thoughtful man who enjoyed racing his dirt bike across the desert. He worked as a mental health professional. When Jera and I were dating and about ready to get married, he taught our Sunday school class. He was an amazing servant of God who also taught a home Bible study and served in many leadership roles. He led a counseling ministry at our church. This man was on fire for Jesus.

And there was Ken, a businessman who led several companies and consulted for others. He built a reputation for wise counsel throughout the business community. Ken was a big man with a big heart for God, the gospel, and the church. He was a great Bible teacher and man of prayer. He served with distinction as an elder for many years. In Africa, he risked his life to help people hear about Jesus. He did what was best for the church even when it did not seem best for him. He walked with Jesus and loved his church.

If these men had gotten together and given me a million dollars, that money would not have been anywhere near as valuable to me as the consistent example they lived out before me.

LOVE FOR CHRIST INCLUDES
LOVE FOR HIS CHURCH

Early in my walk with God, I looked at these men and asked, "Why are they so different? Why do they love the church? Why do they sacrificially give their time, energy, and money? Why do they pour in the effort? I came to understand that their love for Christ encompassed a love for His church.

Today, many Christians mock the church. Some of them resent the church, and even hate it. Perhaps they were hurt, misled, or disappointed. They forget that the church consists of people, and people often hurt, mislead, and disappoint others.

A local church may be a long way from where it should be, but it remains the center of the greatest, most important thing going on in the world. When a church gathers, its people can experience Jesus' presence in special, unique, and powerful ways—all because they are focused wholly on pursuing Jesus Christ.

33

SEVEN REASONS MEN NEED TO LOVE THE CHURCH

H ave you ever thought about the fact you are called to love the church? Perhaps church has been more or less of a place where you go to hear the Word taught and participate in certain kinds of activities. Maybe church has been more functional for you, a place where you seek to have your needs met. But church is far more than that. You're a living part of a group of people who minister to one another and care for one another. You have a role in making your church what it is.

God desires for us to love the church, and here are the reasons:

1. JESUS LOVES THE CHURCH

Ephesians 5:25 says, "Husbands, love your wives, just as Christ also loved the church and gave Himself up for her." Notice how lovingly Jesus views the church. He compares His love for the church to marital love.

We live in the day of the independent evangelical Christian. A 2016 episode of NBC's *The Voice* featured a singer called Sundance

Head, who sang a version of a 1972 song by Tom T. Hall. The song, "Me and Jesus," expresses Christianity as rugged individualism. The song speaks of an individual who chooses to remain independent of godly people encouraging, teaching, exhorting, correcting, helping, counseling, and modeling how to honor God and live well.

Jesus established the church. It is His creation for His glory. If you have your own thing going and it doesn't involve the church, something's wrong.

Jesus is not your sidekick. He's your Lord, which means master. Please know that your salvation rests in Jesus, not the church. But to live a successful and powerful Christian life, you need the church. Jesus made the church because He loves us, and He knows we need each another.

A baby's world centers on self. She delights in playing peekaboo because she's learning that others still exist even when she does not see them. Out of sight, then...*surprise!* Mom still exists. Amazing! Each day a child matures, her world expands further beyond herself.

For Christians, too, increased maturity means seeing a world bigger than yourself. You stop going to church services to be spiritually fed, and you start going so you can help feed others. You don't go there looking for comfort but to comfort. You don't go to be edified, but to edify. Then an amazing thing happens; You go home fed, comforted, and edified.

What happened? You started to love the church the way Jesus loves the church, remembering that the church is made not of bricks and mortar, but people.

Real men love the church because Jesus loves the church!

2. JESUS IS LORD OF THE CHURCH

Let's say you work at Target or Walmart. When you arrive, does anyone use the store's public address system to encourage you in Christ?

I've been at many construction sites and heard the name of Jesus numerous times, but almost never as Lord. In college, professors and students also spoke often of Jesus, but again, almost never as Lord.

The church is different. At church, it's not at all inappropriate or uncommon to hear someone say, "Jesus is Lord!" Ephesians 1:22-23 says, "He put all things in subjection under His feet, and gave Him as head over all things to the church, which is His body, the fullness of Him who fills all in all." This is not some theological platitude. Jesus is Lord everywhere. But in the church, we acknowledge this truth, seek to understand it, and encourage one another to submit to Him as Lord in our lives.

The church is the one organization with a perfect leader—Jesus. We fail, but our Leader does not!

3. JESUS EMPOWERS THE CHURCH

We need power to live godly lives. We need power to love our wives and influence our children. We need power to say no to sin and temptation. We need power to "press toward the mark for the prize of the high calling of God in Christ Jesus" (Philippians 3:14 kjv).

If you're reading this book, you have been tempted. In fact, when you picked it up earlier today, you may have been tempted to do something else: Perhaps this thought went through your mind: *This is important stuff, but I can read it later. Right now, my favorite show is on!*

With so many entertainment options available every second of the day, something's always available to pull you away. Satan will work to tempt you in things large and small, and he especially wants to draw your thoughts away from Christ. We talked earlier about the deluge of thoughts that hit us from worldly sources. Those thoughts tend to draw us toward "all that is in the world, the lust of the flesh and the lust of the eyes and the boastful pride of life" (1 John 2:16).

How do you and your children stand up against such an onslaught? Determination will not be enough. Psych yourself up to be good, and you will fall short. You need power straight from the throne of God. Your children need that power too. The church serves as a conduit that provides you and your family power to live uncompromising lives in a wicked world.

In Ephesians 1:18-21, Paul wrote,

> I pray that the eyes of your heart may be enlightened, so that you will know what is the hope of His calling, what are the riches of the glory of His inheritance in the saints, and what is the surpassing greatness of His power toward us who believe. These are in accordance with the working of the strength of His might which He brought about in Christ, when He raised Him from the dead and seated Him at His right hand in the heavenly places, far above all rule and authority and power and dominion, and every name that is named, not only in this age but also in the one to come.

"That the eyes of your heart may be enlightened" is a prayer to end blindness. What are we blind to? This passage lists three areas of blindness common to believers, starting with "the hope of His calling." This is not one of those wishy-washy hopes. This is a sure and certain hope. The world tends to drain hope from you, your wife, your children, and your fellow believers. Pray that the Holy Spirit enlightens your eyes to the hope of the calling that you have in Christ.

We also need enlightenment regarding "the riches of the glory of His inheritance in the saints." By the material standards of the world, you may be tapped out. But you own an inheritance in heaven that is filled with unprecedented, immeasurable riches.

The third part of this prayer is that we see "the surpassing greatness of His power toward us who believe." How glorious! May God give each of us the enlightenment of heart to see "the surpassing greatness of His power" toward us. You can experience His power anywhere, but church helps us to focus on tapping into that power.

On our own, we tend to live in spiritual bondage, denial, and endless loops of sin and defeat. But Jesus provides the power of the Spirit of God so that we can say no to sin and yes to righteousness. He gives us the power to fight, and the power to win!

We need charging up, and we need it regularly. You will find the power of God released regularly *in church*! If you want to tap into the infinite power source, you can do so *in church*!

In church, we tap into God's power.

4. THE CHURCH IS A PLACE FOR DECLARING TRUTH

In 1 Timothy 3:15, Paul said, "I write so that you will know how one ought to conduct himself in the household of God, which is the church of the living God, the pillar and support of the truth."

Modern academics teach children that truth is malleable, and that it can be personalized to excuse any behavior. They talk about "my truth" and "your truth" as though truth changes to fit our specific circumstances.

The church, however, stands on the truth of God, which is unchanging. And what is truth? Jesus defined it in a prayer to His Father in John 17:17: "Your word is truth." In 2 Timothy 4:2, pastors are commanded to preach the Bible, the Word of truth. Scripture tells us that in the last days, people will not want to hear the truth. Instead, they will prefer myths and lies (2 Timothy 4:3-4). The church is the place to seek the God of truth: the truth about origins, meaning, purpose, ethics, life, God, marriage, parenting, finances, good and evil, heaven and hell.

The church of Jesus Christ stands on truth. In John 14:6, Jesus said, "I am...the truth." The church honors Him by honoring the truth and standing on it. As 1 Timothy 3:15 says, the church is "the pillar and support of the truth." It is hard to imagine what is more needed in the world today than truth.

5. JESUS WILL RESCUE THE CHURCH

Jesus has rescued those in the church from the penalty of sin, which is hell. In John 10:11, Jesus said, "I am the good shepherd; the good shepherd lays down His life for the sheep."

The good shepherd does something else too. He rescues the sheep from danger. The Bible warns of a coming period of tribulation. The book of Revelation describes this time with great detail. It will be global, unprecedented, and cataclysmic. First Thessalonians 1:10 says that Jesus "rescues us [the church] from the wrath to come."

Jesus does not save or rescue businesses, banks, cars, or homes. He rescues His church—His people. Are you one of His people? Are you one of His children?

6. THE CHURCH IS JESUS' PROGRAM

Churches always seem to be on the lookout for new and better programs. Sincere people want to do great and noble things for God and change the world. But we don't need new programs; we already have what we need: the church. Take some time to read the book of Acts, and you'll see what I mean. It was *the church* that preached the gospel, comforted the afflicted, helped the poor, and changed the world.

Several years ago, I began to understand the Lord's deep concern for orphans. Soon after that, I helped start an orphanage in Uganda. Four years later, the ministry was caring for a couple hundred children. It was great, but it was not Jesus' plan. I came to realize that the local churches in Uganda could care for orphans better than an orphanage, so I shifted my efforts toward helping the local churches to connect with the ministry.

We helped those local churches create cottage businesses so they could care for themselves and the children. We did not need a new program. We needed to use the one Jesus had already put in place—the church. The church is His program for impacting the world.

7. JESUS BUILDS HIS CHURCH AND THE GATES OF HELL WILL NOT PREVAIL AGAINST IT

Jesus said, "I will build my church; and the gates of Hades will not overpower it" (Matthew 16:18). He spoke those words to the disciples at Caesarea Philippi while they were overlooking a pagan temple. I have stood there many times, thinking about what the disciples were viewing as they heard Jesus' words. They beheld an ornate Roman temple in all its grandeur, and yet Jesus did not even own a home (let alone a temple). What a contrast!

Jesus was right. The temple, with its glory and fame, has long since been destroyed. But the church of Jesus continues to march on around the globe 2,000 years later. Nothing can stop the true church, Jesus' people—not Satan, false teachers, governments, persecution, or COVID-19.

Humanity makes many wonderful and beautiful things: cars, planes, ships, homes, buildings, companies, nonprofits, and much more. That's good. God made humans to be builders for a purpose. But know this: At some point, all these things will pass away or come under the authority of the Antichrist—including that beautiful, venerable church building.

Make your sacrifices and hard work last; be a church man. Commit yourself to strengthening the church, and you will not be disappointed.

Jesus intends for His church to do more than just exist. His plan is for His church to be strong, vibrant, and dynamic. He plans to use men just like you to make that happen. Unfortunately, many men are spiritually passive. And churches wither when men do not follow the Man Code.

God has called men to

- pursue biblical success
- possess focused ambition
- assume responsibility
- exhibit godly character
- demonstrate consideration
- protect others
- work with diligence
- respect authority
- honor their wives
- train their children

Everything falls apart when men

- abandon their families
- stop loving the gospel and the church

Be a church man! Real men love both the gospel and the church.

STUDY QUESTIONS

1. What is the gospel of Jesus, the Christ?

2. Why is the gospel so important? How does it change your life?

3. Can you know for sure that you have everlasting life? (see 1 John 5:13).

4. If the gospel is clear and simple, why do so many people stop believing and sharing it, and abandon it?

5. Why are the church and local churches essential?

6. Who is the head (the final authority) of the church and the local church?

7. The church and God's Word are inextricably linked. Without the Bible, on what does the church stand?

8. Of the people you have known in life, does anyone stand out as a role model for you? Why? And what kind of role model are you to others?

9. Are you reluctant to pour yourself fully into a local church? If so, what's holding you back? Why is your involvement so important?

A CALL TO ACTION

Everyone needs a code to live by. It provides clarity for one's own life. It binds the like-minded together. It defines who we are and what we ought to be. It sets goals for growth and enables us to persevere when the going gets tough. The Man Code has done this for me, my sons, and many others.

Don't be like the many men today who are passive and don't heed God's call on their lives. Take up the Man Code and...

LEARN IT

There is no excuse for failing to follow through. The Man Code is typed up on a cheat sheet in the back of this book. Post the sheet on your mirror, car visor, or computer. Review it every day for 30 days. Find a friend and make him a commitment: "If I cannot recite the Man Code to you in 30 days, I will give you $100." Trust me, everyone will want to be your accountability partner, and you will help him learn the Code too!

Help others learn the Man Code with you. Figure out what motivates them and use it for good in their life. My grandsons each have a standing offer from me. You memorize and quote the 12 points of the Man Code, and you will earn $5 for each point—$60 the first time you recite the list in order. Now the older one cheers the younger ones to man up and get it memorized. For others it might be a fishing trip or tickets to a football game.

If you are a father, I would suggest you not let a young man marry your daughter without him being able to recite the Man Code. Learn it with him and help build it into his life.

LIVE IT

The Man Code is not an academic pursuit. It's not about merely learning facts. I struggled all through my education trying to connect the dots of academia to real life. How is this going to help me during the next 20 years? The Man Code is about the nuts and bolts of real life; it is to be lived. Be successful today—please God! Protect others—your world needs you. Be diligent at work—worship God in that place. Love the gospel—someone you know is going to a Christless eternity. This is about real life. It really matters.

You and I may not change the whole world, but we can change *our* world. Live the Code, and change those around you.

TEACH IT

What have you been passing on to others? What would you like to pass on? Many men pass on things of little value. Some pass on a godless vocabulary, lustful passions, selfishness, and fear. I have known many such men. Some come across as nice guys but live in an unintentional, passive way. Some men stand a bit taller and leave us with a fire within our souls for education, etiquette, work, sports, the arts, or other common pursuits. And a few stand strong like redwood trees, reaching to a whole different level, and pass on the essence of life—being a true man of God.

The Man Code is transferable. It is like a chain saw; it cuts through the brush that has grown over men's souls. It is like the well-driven nails that restore strength to a weak structure. It is like a new coat of paint that refreshes what was fading.

Stand tall. Put some thought into the Man Code. The Lord will give you wisdom. Teach it!

EXPECT IT

You have heard it: "Everyone gets a trophy today for just showing up." How nice. It makes everyone feel so good. *How delusional!*

Jesus gives us a better life principle: To whom much is given, much is required (Luke 12:48). Do you recall Jesus' parable of the talents? (Matthew 25:14-30). It is a story that teaches this spiritual truth. In short, a wealthy man was going on a journey, and he left his three servants with a large sum of money to invest. Each one received an amount according to his ability—not everyone had the same ability. One man received one talent (a talent was about 58 to 80 pounds of silver). Another man received two talents, and the last man received five.

When the owner returned from his long journey and settled accounts, the men who received the two and five talents had worked hard and doubled the owner's assets. They were honored for their efforts. However, the man who received the one talent had buried it—and it produced nothing. When called before the owner, he gave it back, but with no interest. The owner was not impressed. He called this man wicked and lazy (verse 26).

Like the men in the parable, we, too, will give an account to King Jesus for how we use what He has entrusted to us in this life.

Again, catch the principle: To whom much is given, much is required. As a Christian man, God has given you life, a measure of health and intellect, eternal life, and the Holy Spirit. And in Scripture, He has given you the priorities that are laid out in the Man Code. God is expecting you to live a great life, a full life, and a meaningful life. He is expecting to see the Man Code in you.

Therefore, we should expect it of one another. You can, and should, expect it from me. Be assured that I am expecting it of you.

A REAL MAN

"I have another group of guys," Jeff said to me on the phone. He was heading out on another man adventure to the High Sierras. While the men with Jeff were seeking rainbow trout, Jeff was fishing for something much more—them!

Jeff is a successful husband, father, and businessman in Southern California. He is a high-capacity man with a lot of responsibility and a lot of demands. He is driven and successful from a human perspective in every way.

Yet his success runs much deeper and is eternal. Not only has he trusted in Jesus, but he follows Him. Jeff follows Him on mission with the gospel by praying for each of his clients before consultations. Jeff follows Him by protecting vulnerable people in his world of influence. Jeff follows Him by caring for his wife and family's spiritual, emotional, and physical needs. Jeff lives the Man Code before God and others.

His man adventures in the mountains are loaded with purpose. Jeff models and teaches his friends and guests the principles reflected in the Man Code. I am always excited to hear the amazing stories of how God worked on the trip, but the *eternal legacy* that is cultivated in the men is even more powerful! I have no idea how many lives have been transformed through Jeff's ministry, but my trip with him ten years ago was life-changing. When Jeff stands before Christ, be assured he will be honored for knowing the Man Code, living it, teaching it, and expecting it.

Brother, it's your turn! Step up!

To the Code!

THE MAN CODE

12 PRIORITIES EVERY MAN NEEDS TO KNOW

A REAL MAN...

1. Pursues biblical success

2. Possesses focused ambition

3. Assumes responsibility

4. Exhibits godly character

5. Demonstrates consideration

6. Protects others

7. Works with diligence

8. Respects authority

9. Honors his wife

10. Trains his children

11. Does not abandon his family

12. Loves the gospel and the church

NOTES

CHAPTER 1: WE HAVE A CRISIS

1. Nicole M. Fortin, Philip Oreopoulos, Shelley Phipps, "Leaving Boys Behind: Gender Disparities In High Academic Achievement," *National Bureau of Economic Research*, August 2013, http://www.nber.org/papers/w19331.

2. Linda Poon, "Girls Get Good Grades But Still Need Help. As for Boys…SOS," *NPR*, January 29, 2015, https://www.npr.org/sections/goatsandsoda/2015/01/29/382413365/girls-get-good-grades-but-still-need-help-as-for-boys-sos.

3. Dante Chinni, "More women than men have college degrees. That's good news for Democrats," *NBC News*, August 20, 2023, https://www.nbcnews.com/meet-the-press/data-download/women-men-college-degrees-good-news-democrats-rcna100833.

4. Alexandre Tanzi, "U.S. Women Outpacing Men in Higher Education: Demographic Trends," *Bloomberg*, August 6, 2018, https://www.bloomberg.com/news/articles/2018-08-06/u-s-women-outpacing-men-in-higher-education-demographic-trends.

5. Warren Farrell, "The Boy Crisis: A Sobering Look at the State of Our Boys," TEDxMarin, 2016.

6. John Woodrow Cox et al., "More than 357,000 students have experienced gun violence at school since Columbine," *The Washington Post*, October 26, 2023. https://www.washingtonpost.com/education/interactive/school-shootings-database/.

7. "Mental Health by the Numbers," *National Alliance on Mental Illness*, 2021, https://www.nami.org/mhstats.

8. Daniel Patrick Moynihan, "Defining Deviancy Down: How We've Become Accustomed to Alarming Levels of Crime and Destructive Behavior," *American Educator*, Winter 1993/1994, https://nation.time.com/wp-content/uploads/sites/8/2012/03/defining-deviancy-down-amer educator.pdf.

9. Annalies Winny, "Life Expectancy Is Declining in the U.S. It Doesn't Have to Be," *John Hopkins University Bloomberg School*, December 6, 2022, https://publichealth.jhu.edu/2022/life-expectancy-is-declining-in-the-us.

10. Dr. Edith Bracho-Sanchez, "Suicide rates in girls are rising, study finds, especially in those age 10 to 14, *CNN*, updated Monday May 20, 2019, https://www.cnn.com/2019/05/17/health/suicide-rates-young-girls-study/index.html.

11. Jamie Ducharme, "The Gap Between Male and Female Youth Suicide Rates Is Narrowing in the U.S.," *Time*, May 17, 2019, https://time.com/5590344/youth-suicide-rates/.

12. "Suicide Mortality in the United States, 2000-2020," *Centers for Disease Control and Prevention*, https://www.cdc.gov/nchs/products/databriefs/db433.htm.

13. Jack Brewer, "ISSUE BRIEF: Fatherlessness and its effects on American society," *America First Policy Institute*, May 15, 2023, https://americafirstpolicy.com/latest/issue-brief-fatherlessness -and-its-effects-on-american-society.

14. Kristen Rogers, "US teens use screens more than seven hours a day on average—and that's not including school work," *CNN*, October 29, 2019, https://www.cnn.com/2019/10/29/health/ common-sense-kids-media-use-report-wellness/index.html.

15. PsychGuides.com says, "1 in 5 internet searches on a mobile device are for pornography…88% of porn scenes contain physical aggression." According to Webroot, 35% of all internet downloads are related to pornography—"Porn Addiction," *PsychGuides.com*, https://www.psychguides .com/behavioral-disorders/porn-addiction/#:~:text=Pornography%20Statistics&text=1%20 in%205%20internet%20searches,porn%20scenes%20contain%20physical%20aggression . *Psychology Today* reports, "More than 90 percent of young men report watching porn videos with some regularity"—"Porn Addiction," *Psychology Today*, https://www.psychologytoday .com/us/basics/porn-addiction.

16. According to a Kaiser Family Foundation study, "Eight- to eighteen-year-olds spend more time with media than in any other activity besides (maybe) sleeping—an average of more than 7 1/2 hours a day, seven days a week"—"Generation M2: Media in the Lives of 8- to 18-Year-Olds," *Kaiser Family Foundation*, https://www.kff.org/other/event/generation-m2 -media-in-the-lives-of/. Recovery Village reports, "64% of the U.S. population are gamers. The average male gamer is 33 years old…Males between the ages of 18-24 are most at risk for gaming addiction. 94% of males and 6% of females represent the gender breakdown for gaming addiction"—"Video Game Addiction Statistics," *choosingtherapy.com*, https://www .choosingtherapy.com/video-game-addiction/#:~:text=In%20an%20overview%20of%20 current,Recovery%20Village%20reported%20the%20following%3A&text=64%25%20of%20 the%20U.S.%20population,gamer%20is%2037%20years%20old.

17. "Present hedonistic" is one of the time perspectives laid out by Philip Zimbardo, psychologist and professor emeritus at Stanford University.

CHAPTER 2: TO THE (MAN) CODE!

1. As cited in Patrick Dorinson, "Why the Cowboy Code Is Not Frivolous," *Fox News*, February 10, 2011, https://www.foxnews.com/opinion/why-the-cowboy-code-is-not-frivolous.

2. "West Point Cadet Honor Code and Honor System," *United States Military Academy West Point*, https://www.westpoint.edu/military/simon-center-for-the-professional-military-ethic/ honor#:~:text=West%20Point's%20Cadet%20Honor%20Code,or%20tolerate%20those%20 who%20do.%22&text=Here%20is%20a%20brief%20overview,established%20Character%20 Integration%20Advisory%20Group.

3. From a speech Douglas MacArthur gave at West Point two years before his death.

PART 1: REAL MEN PURSUE BIBLICAL SUCCESS

1. From the *Meditations* of Marcus Aurelius.

2. These words are attributed to the Greek philosopher Socrates, who lived circa 470 to 399 BC.

CHAPTER 4: DAVID'S SUCCESS

1. "Personal Protective Equipment: Army and Marine Corps Are Pursuing Efforts to Reduce the Weight of Items Worn or Carried in Combat," *Government Accountability Office*, May 2017, https://www.gao.gov/assets/gao-17-431.pdf.

2. Tim Collins, "Roman sling-bullets used against Scottish tribes 2,000 years ago were as deadly as a .44 Magnum," *The Daily Mail*, May 25, 2017, https://www.dailymail.co.uk/sciencetech/article-4541318/Roman-sling-bullets-deadly-44-Magnum.html#:~:text=Roman%20sling%20bullets%20used%20against,44%20Magnum&text=Tribal%20warriors%20who%20faced%20an,those%20in%20a%20modern%20handgun.

PART 2: REAL MEN POSSESS FOCUSED AMBITION

1. This quote by Bruce Lee is cited in many places, among them being Hal Berman, "Bruce Lee's Secret—Five Focus Lessons from a Master," *Hal Berman*, September 21, 2020, https://www.halberman.com/post/bruce-lee-s-secret-five-focus-lessons-from-a-master.

2. "Biography of Napoleon Bonaparte, Great Military Commander," *ThoughtCo.*, https://www.thoughtco.com/napoleon-bonaparte-biography-1221106.

CHAPTER 6: DEFEATING DISTRACTIONS

1. K. Anders Ericsson et al., "The Making of an Expert," *Harvard Business Review*, July-August 2007, https://hbr.org/2007/07/the-making-of-an-expert.

2. K. Anders Ericsson, "Guest Post: The Danger Of Delegating Education To Journalists," *radical scholarship.com*, November 3, 2014, https://radicalscholarship.com/2014/11/03/guest-post-the-danger-of-delegating-education-to-journalists-k-anders-ericsson/.

CHAPTER 7: THE MAN WHO RESCUED THE WORLD

1. C.S. Lewis, "On Stories" in *Of Other Worlds: Essays and Stories* (New York: Harcourt Brace Jovanovich, 1966), 15. "On Stories" was first published in 1947.

PART 3: REAL MEN ASSUME RESPONSIBILITY

1. From a speech given by Winston Churchill, as cited by the *International Churchill Society*, https://winstonchurchill.org/old-site/learn/speeches-learn/the-price-of-greatness/.

2. From John F. Kennedy's inaugural address on January 20, 1961.

CHAPTER 9: THE MAN WHO RESCUED A WOMAN AND CHANGED A NATION

1. The leaders of ancient nations often made pronouncements regarding their beneficence to the poor, but the laws almost never made actual provision for them.

PART 4: REAL MEN EXHIBIT GODLY CHARACTER

1. This quote is widely attributed to Abraham Lincoln—original source unknown.

2. As cited at "Benjamin Franklin's Famous Quotes," *The Franklin Institute*, https://www.fi.edu/en/benjamin-franklin/famous-quotes#:~:text=%E2%80%9CWhat%20more%20valuable%20than%20Gold,Virtue.%E2%80%9D.

CHAPTER 10: DEVELOPING AND DEPLOYING CHARACTER

1. If you are a woman or girl reading this, don't feel left out. The principles in Proverbs also pertain to you.

2. Maria Campbell and James Freeman Clarke, *Revolutionary Services and Civil Life of General William Hull* (New York: D. Appleton & Company, 1848), 265-266.

3. Jon Simpson, "Finding Brand Success in the Digital World," *Forbes*, August 25, 2017, https://www.forbes.com/sites/forbesagencycouncil/2017/08/25/finding-brand-success-in-the-digital-world/.

CHAPTER 11: CHARACTER IN THE FURNACE

1. People often hear the story of Shadrach, Meshach, and Abed-nego and wonder where Daniel was during the events of their encounter with the fiery furnace. Daniel was a high-ranking official in the Babylonian Empire, and the empire was huge. It covered much of what we now call the Middle East. There were no telegraphs, telephones, or emails. It makes sense, then, that Daniel was probably traveling on empire business at the time of his friends' trouble in Babylon. He probably would not have known about the events in his province until weeks after they occurred. And even if he had known, travel back would have taken a long time.

2. Robert Francis Harper, "The Biblical World: Nebuchadnezzar, King of Babylon," University of Chicago, July 1899.

PART 5: REAL MEN DEMONSTRATE CONSIDERATION

1. This quote is widely attributed to Bryant McGill—original source unknown.

2. Booker T. Washington, *Up from Slavery: An Autobiography*, Project Gutenberg eBook, https://www.gutenberg.org/cache/epub/2376/pg2376-images.html.

CHAPTER 12: CONSIDERATION AND TRUTH

1. The NLT is especially helpful in showing that Titus led a group of brothers in the Lord who "bring honor to Christ."

2. Alan Tacca, "Easter 2020: Is a quieter God in control?," *Daily Monitor*, April 12, 2020, https://www.monitor.co.ug/uganda/oped/columnists/allan-tacca/easter-2020-is-a-quieter-god-in-control--1884956.

CHAPTER 13: THREE KINDS OF CONSIDERATION

1. Alexa Mellardo, "10 Of The Sexiest Things A Guy Can Do That Have Nothing To Do With Sex," *Elite Daily*, April 14, 2016, https://www.elitedaily.com/dating/how-to-be-sexy/1457052.

2. Regina Corso, "Three in Five Americans Say U.S. Has Long Way to Go to Reach Gender Equality," *The Harris Poll*, August 16, 2010, http://multivu.prnewswire.com/mnr/harrisinteractive/44727/.

3. Emily Esfahani Smith, "Let's Give Chivalry Another Chance," *The Atlantic*, December 10, 2012, https://www.theatlantic.com/sexes/archive/2012/12/lets-give-chivalry-another-chance/266085/.

4. *Chicago Record Herald*, Sunday, April 21, 2012.

PART 6: REAL MEN PROTECT OTHERS

1. Jeff Cooper, *The Art of the Rifle* (Boulder, CO: Paladin Press, 1997), 10.

CHAPTER 14: PROTECTOR

1. Adam Gabbatt, "New Hampshire man chokes to death coyote who attacked toddler," *The Guardian*, January 21, 2020, https://www.theguardian.com/us-news/2020/jan/21/new-hampshire-coyote-choke-death-toddler.

2. Ian Janssen, Steven B. Heymsfield, ZiMian Wang, and Robert Ross, "Skeletal muscle mass and distribution in 468 men and women aged 18-88," *Journal of Applied Psychology* (July 1, 2000), 89(1): 81-88.

3. A.E. Miller et al., "Gender differences in strength and muscle fiber characteristics," *European Journal of Applied Physiology and Occupational Physiology* (1993), 66(3): 254-62.

PART 7: REAL MEN WORK WITH DILIGENCE

1. As cited in Ryan Yuenger, "First-year Bay City Western coach instills motto used by Kevin Durant, Tim Tebow," *MLive*, April 6, 2016, https://www.mlive.com/staff/ryuenger/posts.html.

2. This quote is widely attributed to Colin Powell—original source unknown.

CHAPTER 18: GOD AND WORK

1. "Slave societies," *Britannica*, https://www.britannica.com/topic/slavery-sociology/The-law-of-slavery.

2. "The Roman Empire in the First Century," *PBS*, https://www.pbs.org/empires/romans/empire/slaves_freemen.html#:~:text=In%20hard%20times%2C%20it%20was,selling%20their%20children%20into%20slavery.&text=All%20slaves%20and%20their%20families,whipped%2C%20branded%20or%20cruelly%20mistreated.

3. "Food Waste FAQs," *US Department of Agriculture*, https://www.usda.gov/foodwaste/faqs.

4. "New FDA Food Code Reduces Barriers to Food Donations," *US Food and Drug Administration*, February 14, 2023, https://www.fda.gov/food/cfsan-constituent-updates/new-fda-food-code-reduces-barriers-food-donations.

PART 8: REAL MEN RESPECT AUTHORITY

1. H.W. Crocker III, *Robert E. Lee on Leadership* (Washington, DC: Regnery, 1999), 172.

CHAPTER 19: UNDERSTANDING AUTHORITY

1. "World Watch List 2023: More than 360m Christians suffer high levels of persecution and discrimination for their faith," *Open Doors*, 2003, https://www.opendoors.org/en-US/persecution/countries/.

CHAPTER 20: SUBJECT TO MEN, PROTECTED BY GOD

1. Patrick Ryan, "Top 10 Evil People From Ancient Times," *ListVerse*, May 30, 2012, https://listverse.com/2012/05/30/top-10-evil-people-from-ancient-times/.

CHAPTER 22: THE MAN WHO SUBMITTED AND RULED

1. This may have been another name for Cyrus the Persian.

PART 9: REAL MEN HONOR THEIR WIVES

1. Martin H. Manser, *The Westminster Collection of Christian Quotations* (Louisville, KY: Westminster John Knox Press, 2001), 240.

2. Dave Willis, Facebook post on May 6, 2017, https://www.facebook.com/davewillis78/posts/great-marriages-dont-happen-by-luck-or-by-accident-they-are-the-result-of-a-cons/1856591827998213/.

CHAPTER 24: REFLECTIONS FOR SINGLES

1. Jerri Menges, "Tony Evans Presses On," *Decision*, July 20, 2021, https://decisionmagazine.com/tony-evans-presses-on/.

PART 10: REAL MEN TRAIN THEIR CHILDREN

1. From an address given by Franklin D. Roosevelt at University of Pennsylvania on September 20, 1940, https://www.presidency.ucsb.edu/documents/address-university-pennsylvania.

2. Matthew Henry, *Matthew Henry's Commentary*, 2 Samuel, chapter 13, verses 1-20, *Bible Gateway*, https://www.biblegateway.com/resources/matthew-henry/2Sam.13.1-2Sam.13.20.

CHAPTER 26: TWELVE AREAS OF TRAINING

1. John 1:3 explains that Jesus created everything.

PART 11: REAL MEN DO NOT ABANDON THEIR FAMILIES

1. This quote is widely attributed to Ronald Oliver—original source unknown.

CHAPTER 29: DIVORCE

1. Bradley R.E. Wright, *Christians Are Hate-Filled Hypocrites...and Other Lies You've Been Told: A Sociologist Shatters Myths from the Secular and Christian Media* (Minneapolis, MN: Bethany House, 2010), 133.

2. To learn more about marriage vows, read 1 Corinthians 7:10-16, 25-40.

CHAPTER 30: "WHAT GOD HAS JOINED TOGETHER"

1. There are obviously cases when one spouse can no longer physically have intercourse. That person is not condemned, and it does not give his or her spouse a license to "shop around." Life is complicated. Get wise counsel. Seek God's grace to love your spouse and be faithful to God and him or her.

PART 12: REAL MEN LOVE THE GOSPEL AND THE CHURCH

1. Kevin DeYoung, "Reaching the Next Generation: Hold Them with Holiness," *The Gospel Coalition*, October 21, 2009, https://www.thegospelcoalition.org/blogs/kevin-deyoung/reaching-the-next-generation-hold-them-with-holiness/.

To learn more about Harvest House books and
to read sample chapters, visit our website:

www.HarvestHousePublishers.com

HARVEST HOUSE PUBLISHERS
EUGENE, OREGON